SELF-DEFENSE
FOR WOMEN

about the authors

While in college, Donald Monkerud studied fencing and boxing. After graduation from San Diego State University, he studied Goju-Ryu Karate for two years with Gosei Yamaguchi, 8th degree black belt.

He began studying Aikido in 1972, making a trip to Japan to study with Michio Hikitsuchi, 10th degree black belt. His instructors have included Koichi Tohei, former 10th degree black belt and chief instructor at Aikido World Headquarters in Tokyo; Aikira Tohei, 8th degree black belt from Chicago and Tokyo; and Frank Doran, 4th degree black belt and an instructor at San Francisco. Currently, he holds the rank of shodan and has instructed in the Santa Cruz Recreation Department, at the Watsonville YMCA and the University of California/Santa Cruz.

A free-lance writer since 1972, he served as technical editor and writer for SELF DEFENSE WORLD magazine and has written many articles for such magazines as BLACK BELT, KARATE ILLUSTRATED, FIGHTING ARTS and ORIENTAL ARTS on both martial arts and related cultural subjects. He is currently working as contributing editor to Volleyball Magazine, is a former editor for RUNNER'S WORLD, THE MARATHONER and ON THE RUN, and has written chapters for THE COMPLETE DIET GUIDE FOR RUNNERS AND OTHER ATHLETES, GUIDE TO LONG DISTANCE RUNNING and THE COMPLETE MARATHONER. He is writing several books from his home near Santa Cruz.

Mary Heiny earned her BA degree in Japanese at the University of Washington. It was during her time as an exchange student at Keio University, Japan, that she first became interested in Aikido. She began her studies of this martial art at Aikido World Headquarters, Tokyo, in 1968. She trained there five years before returning to the U.S. to teach. Today she holds the rank of 4th degree black belt. She first taught Aikido at the University of California, Santa Cruz in 1974, at that time also conducting a woman's self defense course. In 1976 she opened her own school, The Seattle School of Aikido.

Ms. Heiny is a member of the United States Aikido Federation Board of Governors and is active in teaching at her own school and in workshops around the country.

SELF-DEFENSE FOR WOMEN

Physical Education Activities Series

DONALD MONKERUD

and

MARY HEINY

wcb
Wm. C. Brown Company Publishers
Dubuque, Iowa

Consulting Editors

Physical Education—Aileene Lockhart
Texas Woman's University

Health—Robert Kaplan
The Ohio State University

Parks and Recreation—David Gray
California State University, Long Beach

Physical Education Activities

Evaluation Materials Editor
Jane A. Mott
Texas Woman's University

Copyright © 1980 by Wm. C. Brown Company Publishers

Library of Congress Catalog Card Number: 79-54137

ISBN 0-697-07082-4

Printed in the United States of America

contents

acknowledgments

Special thanks to the people who helped make this book possible: Marc Gabriel; Carol Hamilton; Linda Henry; Carrie Kersten; Steve Kersten; Vicki Kersten; Lizzy Lynn; Dan Silvea; Tom Tutko; Jim Williamson; Frank Doran, fourth dan, Aikido; Keiko Fukuda, sixth dan, Kodokan; Michio Hitkitsuchi, tenth dan, Aikido; and Gosei Yamaguchi, chief instructor, Goju-Kai Karata-Do, USA. Photography by Dave Madison.

women and violence

1

In part our society exists in a complex, urbanized environment. Some places are safe and secure, others are dangerous. By spending a few minutes you can recall several possible threats of physical danger to yourself. We are all aware of common dangers in our daily lives—a child's toys on a stairway, a frayed electrical plug in the home, a hot pan of oil on the stove. Other dangers may be a bald tire or faulty brakes on your car or a gas leak in your heating stove. All these situations make an accident possible. The dangers may come from a physical source and threaten material harm to your body.

But there are other dangers that are not so obvious and that are often overlooked. Recently in a self-defense workshop, we asked for a show of hands of the number of people who had physical confrontations or fights within the past six months. Two of the sixty people raised their hands. Then we asked for an indication of those who had been made physically ill, depressed, uncomfortable, or mentally affected by other people in the past six months. Almost three-quarters of the class raised their hands.

Alerting oneself to danger signals of all kinds is an important self defense measure. How many warnings of potential trouble can you think of that might be found in a home bathroom?

Upon closer examination, our notions of "self-defense" seem somewhat limited. Before you can learn to deal with an actual physical attack, you need to expand your concepts of danger and self-defense to include many areas of your life that you may have overlooked or neglected up to this time. If you think only of physical defense against an attack, you will be limited to notions of fighting and how to use your muscular skill and force to overcome an attacker. This one aspect of self-defense is often less important than many psychological aspects are.

Generally speaking, we may say that protecting ourselves from danger encompasses both the mental and the physical. But self-defense actually begins with mental attitudes and psychological orientation. In the past, social norms have created many psychological barriers to a woman's ability to defend herself. A woman is often taught to feel guilty if she says "No" to someone, always to let the other person have his way, to remain silent, to allow herself to be coerced, or to let others take responsibility for her. Thus psychological mechanisms are set in motion that ultimately become harmful. Emotional disturbances can lead to ignoring physical dangers; or such feelings may be internalized, resulting in reactions like anxiety, nervousness, loss of appetite, insomnia, and general restlessness.

Culturally both men and women have been trained to feel regret or remorse if they deny someone else's wishes, to feel sad if they disappoint someone else, or to become depressed when things don't go the way they plan. Depression, apprehension and sadness can condition your responses and trap you in your own emotions. Depression leads to further depression and disappointment.

Psychologists tell us that one of the signs of a healthy individual is the ability to see various options and different ways of solving problems.[1] Mentally ill individuals, for example, perceive fewer choices when faced with problems in their lives. The same may be said for a normal, healthy person when he or she is not feeling well or is depressed. One student's parents would not allow her to take a job because she would get off late at night when conditions were not safe. But the student found there was a taxi that would pick her up and bring her safely home. If she had become depressed she probably wouldn't have thought of alternatives. Thinking of other possibilities will often allow you to protect yourself from mental anxiety and disappointment. If a boss becomes angry at you, you might internalize his criticism and feel bad. In reality, his anger may have little to do with you. The employer or manager may have had an argument with someone else and be taking it out on you, or he may have a headache. If you made a mistake, of course you want to correct it; but what is done is already finished. All you can do is attempt to be aware the next time and not make the same error twice. If you worry about past mistakes, this may only cause you to make more mistakes in the present. Understanding all the possibilities and finding alternatives can broaden your understanding and help you protect yourself against mental hang-ups.

The mental and physical are closely intertwined, so that it is often difficult to differentiate them. One of the most important factors in protecting yourself from physical dangers and accidents is mental awareness and alertness concerning yourself, other people, and your surrounding environment. This awareness allows you to perceive dangerous situations and to prevent them from affecting you. If you look at the tires when you get gas or notice that the brakes aren't working properly, you can take the car into the shop and have them repaired. If the lock on your apartment door breaks and you ignore it, the lock won't work if you need it. If you are alert, you can get the landlord to fix it immediately. The mental alertness you often take for granted protects you from common dangers.

1. William Glasser, M.D., *Positive Addiction* (New York: Harper & Row, 1976), p. 62.

In a situation where you must defend yourself against violence, training in physical techniques will certainly be helpful. The techniques presented here are easily learned ways of escape and counterattack that do not rely upon your physical strength being greater than an attacker's.

You will strive to keep a situation from going so far that you need to rely upon self-defense techniques. Just because you know safety precautions if a tire blows out on the freeway doesn't mean that you are going to drive with a bald tire and take your chances. Your awareness, alertness, and anticipation are much more valuable in your self-defense, both mental and physical, than is knowing how to fight.

Awareness, alertness, and anticipation must be learned. In the Victorian age, men were supposed to care for women and protect them from physical dangers. Everyday menaces, such as the dangers of an unsafe vehicle or household hazards, were taught by fathers to sons or learned through experience. With the increasing complexity of life in our homes and cities and the weakening ties of the family, much of this experience is not passed from parents to child. Today women must learn to anticipate dangers in the home as well as physical violence.

No longer are women willing to sit back and accept a restricted or passive role in the home and in society. Attitudes of both men and women are changing, a fact that helps women take their place as equals in society. New laws and greater economic freedoms are opening up new possibilities in positions traditionally denied to women. Social and cultural opportunities are having a profound impact on women's roles and self-concepts. Women are learning that often their own conditioning is the only thing standing between them and their desired places in the world, work place and in society as a whole.

SOCIETY AND VIOLENCE

When our society was made up of rural towns and close-knit city communities where many persons knew each other, violence was more predictable and less prevalent. Unfortunately, our society has become a more violent place to live. From 1963 to 1973, crimes increased 174 percent, increasing sixteen times faster than the population. If we look at the FBI Uniform Crime Report statistics broken down into categories, we find that from 1969 to 1974: murder increased 40 percent, rape 49 percent, aggravated assault 47 percent, and robbery increased 48 percent. Law enforcement officials state that many more crimes go unreported.[2] The victims don't feel the police can do anything, they are embarassed to report the crime, or they simply don't want to be bothered.

Although many sociologists and criminologists are studying the causes of crime, they do not have any final answers concerning what has caused the drastic increases in crime. Actually the causes are myriad and interlocking. Increasing urbanization accompanied by alienation and weakening family

---

2. Federal Bureau of Investigation, *Uniform Crime Reports*, 1963-1974.

ties are certainly factors. Racial inequality, unemployment, deterioration of the inner city, and rising expectations have all played their roles. Researchers will require many more years to pinpoint the causes and develop solutions to the increasing violence in society.

The victims of crime are legion in today's society. Are you personally acquainted with anyone who has been robbed or assaulted within the past year? Can you think of measures that might have prevented the crime?

Increasingly, women are as often victims of crime as are men. Burglary and armed robbery may strike men or women. Purse snatching is increasing. In the past assault was a crime committed by men against other men. Today women too are being assaulted in small but significant numbers; they are no longer immune to crimes of violence. As women participate more fully in public, economic, and social life, they need to recognize attendant dangers and take precautions to prevent becoming victims of crime.

In the Victorian age women were sheltered and did not discuss or think about themselves being the victims of violent crime. But today whoever reads the newspaper or watches the news knows that violence can affect young and old, rich or poor, and male or female, at any time or place. While women are victims of all categories of crime, the specific crime of rape is increasing at an alarming pace. When thoughts, feelings, and discussion of sex was prohibited during Victorian times, rape was thought of as a sexual crime against a man's property. Today the crime is being seen for what it is—a crime of violence againt a woman. The FBI Uniform Crime Reports reveal forcible rape is "one of the most under-reported crimes, due primarily to fear and/or embarrassment on the part of the victim."[3] Different studies indicate that one in five or possibly one in twenty rapes may actually be reported.[4]

These figures of rising crime rates are not presented to instill fear or to restrict your social life. Everyone needs to be aware, and reminded occasionally, that automobile accidents are real and that they could happen to you. Such awareness leads to greater alertness, taking precautions, and safe driving. Alertness, anticipation, and precautions apply to personal safety. Purse snatching, assault, or rape are not pleasant things to think about. But if you deny that they could happen to you, you may neglect your security and take chances that could lead to an unpleasant experience.

Crimes of violence and rape against women are a deep-rooted social problem. In the long run, they must be dealt with and solved on a mass social and legal basis. At the present time, solutions are being tried but the final solutions appear to lie hidden in the distant future. In the absence of final answers, the responsibility for personal safety falls on the individual woman; she should know how to avoid danger and to defend herself if necessary.

---

3. FBI, *Uniform Crime Reports*, 1973, p. 15.
4. Menachem Amir, *Patterns in Forcible Rape* (Chicago: University of Chicago Press, 1971), p. 27-28.

THE SOCIALIZATION OF WOMEN AND VIOLENCE

Many women do not learn to defend themselves because they feel they do not have the strength and physical abilities. Others may be anxious and uncomfortable thinking about the subject.

Cultural stereotypes and women's social training can be barriers to their defending themselves against violence. Most attitudes toward fear and violence are linked to concepts of male and female, boy and girl, man and woman. From an early age, social values placed on being masculine or feminine affect behavior for the rest of peoples' lives. Men are supposed to be aggressive, to take risks, to compete, and to conquer. Women are supposed to be sedate, humble, demure, and submissive. This social classification begins in the family where the father is the cultural stereotype of a strong authority figure. The mother supports him with love and deference. The family is the immediate conveyor of society's rules, roles, and expectations. Schools, religion, and the popular culture has reinforced these lessons in order to train women in "proper" behavior.

When confronted with the threat of violence or a man's force, the woman has been socially conditioned to yield. Unprepared, defenseless, and passive, she has been trained to believe she is at another's mercy. Dormant in her mind, this conditioning may lead to her defeat and possible injury.

Studies reveal that too many women conform to their social training when facing an attacker. Menachem Amir's study of rape in Philadelphia attempted to measure victim resistance to rape on a statistical basis. Amir found that 55 percent of the rape victims displayed what he termed submissive behavior. Only 27 percent fought back by kicking, hitting, or throwing objects. An initial stranglehold, verbal threats, or the display of a weapon simply paralyzed some women. In 77 percent of the instances considered, men who threatened women with weapons like guns or knives were able to elicit submissive behavior. It appears that terror destroys a woman's rational response to a threat of physical abuse.[5]

The usual advice offered by many men is to tell women they won't be able to defend themselves against physical attack. Such advice is irrational. In the first place, alertness, awareness, and anticipation take no physical strength and can prevent many disasters from occurring. If the situation cannot be prevented, there are many self-defense techniques that do not rely upon strength; using leverage, surprise, and inflicting pain, a woman can escape from or injure her assailant.

No longer willing to accept cultural stereotypes, women are beginning to participate in sports at an earlier age; they are learning that they can and will hurt someone if they need to protect themselves. Women now realize that they can be independent, self-confident, self-reliant, and still be attractive and feminine. But they are also recognizing that the need for defense against physical force or violence as well as from mental intimidation is an absolute necessity in today's complex society.

5. Ibid. pp. 166-71, 226.

MYTHS ABOUT WOMEN AND VIOLENCE

The more a woman understands the cultural and social reasons behind harassment and aggression, the more she will be able to prevent certain situations from developing into violence and physical assault. The stranger on the subway and the leering sidewalk lecher are playing out their cultural stereotypes. But the woman's role is not to be an individual Florence Nightingale (another stereotype) administering to men's needs. Awareness of these cultural roles and behavior can allow you to identify potentially dangerous men and stay away from them.

You will want to be able to handle a situation with the potential for violence. In circumstances where you feel there is a possibility of physical violence to you, the best course of action is to remove yourself immediately from the scene.

Violence exists potentially in many social situations. Salesmen who badger women into buying unwanted merchandise, casual hassling on the street, and the overly familiar bore at a party are less extreme examples of violence or attempts to take advantage of women. Because so many situations are subjective or individual, there is no way to comprehend adequately all situations. Rape is the only type of violence against women that has been studied extensively, and that only recently. Examining the facts and myths about rape will provide insights into other forms of harassment, violence, and serious altercations, thus providing some clues for avoiding such trouble.

Why

The myth of the male being unable to control his passion and pouncing on a stranger has little to do with reality. Rape is not a sexually motivated crime, it is an assault against a woman.

Can you name four common myths about rape?

Researchers do not know exactly what causes a man to rape.[6] They have, however, suggested two broad categories. The first is the masculine roles of strength and aggression carried a step further. Unless held within acceptable limits by concern for others and by sensitivity, aggressiveness can become hard, insistent, cold, and brutal. This macho male becomes fearful of softness or sensitivity in himself. Women threaten his self-concept of masculinity, so that it becomes necessary to strike out against women to destroy the feelings of concern and softness within himself. This type of man hates women and sees in them an outlet for his hostility.[7]

---

6. Carolyn J. Hursch, *The Trouble with Rape* (Chicago: Nelson-Hall, 1977), p. 39.

7. Andrea Medea and Kathleen Thompson, *Against Rape* (New York: Farrar, Straus and Giroux, 1974), p. 23.

The second type of threat comes from a man who threatens, cajoles, intimidates, or overpowers a woman. This man forces himself on a woman by encountering her in a compromising position. The woman is viewed as a sex object, and rape is a way the man attempts to fulfill his identity. Such a confrontation rarely involves brutality or overt violence. This form of rape is more confusing because it often involves a date, a friend, or acquaintance.[8]

Rape between people who know each other is the most difficult to deal with. Often the man is quite normal in other respects. He rapes or pressures a woman into sex against her will because he has her alone and thinks nobody else will find out. The woman feels humiliated, defeated, and violated. Afterwards she may feel guilty because she trusted the man and did not protect herself better. These women make up most unreported rapes; often their attitudes toward themselves and sex are seriously damaged. It is important that after such an experience a woman have counseling, either from a private or state service.

Cultural myths exert untenable pressures on women. One myth asserts, "All women want to be raped." Because so many men have rape fantasies, the "All women want to be raped" myth may be the complement to a male fantasy. The men assume women must be opposites of men. Lacking any physical resistance, some men may assume women like to be brutalized. The problem is that women are receiving the brunt of the pain, humiliation, and social criticism.

"She was asking for it," is a second myth that is associated with few other crimes.[9] The robber seldom blames his victim for the crime. A study in Sing Sing prison in 1955 showed that 80 percent of the prison's rapists were evasive and blamed their victims.[10] This rationalization represents a plea by the rapist not to be prosecuted for his crime. The fact that so many men place the blame on the woman often represents cultural stereotypes, such as the argument that the women should have stayed home behind locked doors and not gone out alone. This plea is paradoxical, because many women are raped in the home.

A study by the Queen's Bench Foundation in San Francisco, entitled "Rape: Prevention and Resistance," sheds some light on why the rapist chooses a particular victim. The subjects for this study were convicted rapists serving time in prison for their offenses. Attractiveness had little to do with their attacks. The men reported the women were merely there, and the attackers perceived them as vulnerable and defenseless. Fifty-two percent were looking for a victim. Almost half had an argument or fight with a wife or girlfriend beforehand. Seventy-six percent reported that they had a recent

---

8. Ibid., p. 24.

9. Susan Brownmiller, *Against Our Will: Men, Women and Rape* (New York: Simon and Schuster, 1975), p. 312.

10. Bernard Gleuck, "Final Report, Research Project for the Study and Treatment of Persons Convicted of Crimes Involving Sexual Aberations," submitted to the Governor of New York, 1965, p. 303.

disappointment leading to a high level of frustration, anger, and depression, which most felt was related to the cause of their crime.[11]

Another reason for holding women accountable for rape is the masculine viewpoint imposed on a woman's experience. The man's response is "Why didn't she fight?" or "How could she be so naive?" or "I would never have let it happen." The men who serve as police, judges, and juries see the women's position from their masculine viewpoint. They can't understand the woman's experience. Men are trained to be assertive, powerful, and aggressive, and too many of them blame the woman for not behaving as men would act in the same situation.

Such myths are being rejected by women who find the cause of rape in the power relationships of the culture. Susan Brownmiller in her book, *Against Our Will: Men, Women, and Rape* says, "From prehistoric times to the present, I believe, rape has played a critical function. It is nothing more or less than a conscious process of intimidation by which all men keep all women in a state of fear."[12]

Who, Where, When

The current image of the rapist is that of a psychopath overcome by sexual deprivation or a dominating mother; however, this myth is refuted by FBI statistics. In psychological tests the vast majority of convicted rapists are indistinguishable from ordinary men.[13]

Neither are these rapist strangers lurking in dark alleys. Menachim Amir found that fifty percent of the rapist he studied were known by the women. Andra Medea and Kathleen Thompson's study of rape in Chicago found thirty-seven percent of the rapes initiated by men who were acquaintances, twenty percent by dates, friends and ex-lovers. Forty-three percent knew the attackers by sight or not at all. The National Commission on the Causes and Prevention of Violence reports that only fifty-three percent of all rape victims were total strangers. Experts consider the number of unreported rapes where the attacker is a friend or acquaintance is much higher.

Following this trend, rapes often occur under ordinary circumstances with over half occurring in the home, a quarter outside in streets, alleys and parks, ten percent in cars and the rest in commercial establishments. Although large cities are more violent generally and rapes more often are committed from July through September, rape and assault are year around activities.

Because the prospects of rape are so terrifying to some women, they readily submit for fear of losing their lives.

11. Queen's Bench Foundation, *Rape: Prevention and Resistance* (San Francisco: Queen's Bench Foundation, 1976), p. 70.

12. Brownmiller, *Against Our Will*, p. 15.

13. Bernard Glueck, "Final Report Research Project for the Study and Treatment of Crimes Involving Sexual Aberations," Minnesota, 1952-55, p. 32.

Fear for one's life is not necessarily a rational response, but it appears when one is under stress. The rapist who murders is relatively rare. In New York City in 1973, there were 1,466 murders. The New York Police Department sex crimes analysis squad reported 3735 rapes and attempted rapes. There were only 28 rape-murders, indicating that less than 1 percent of the rapes included murder.[14] An understanding that rapists seldom murder their victims dispells the myth that women cannot fight back or they will be killed.

The Queen's Bench study is the first to investigate the relationship between completed and attempted rapes, or how resistance affects brutality. The study found that most victims of rape or attempted rape were not seriously injured. Intensified violence correlated with victim resistance, and more victims of complete rape were more severly injured than were attempted rape victims. Although 75 percent of the victims described numbing fear or panic at the inception of the attack, only 51 percent of the intended victims mentioned this response. Ninety percent of the victims remembered being advised to submit. Eighty-eight percent of the women who escaped rape thought of resistance rather than submission.[15] The most important conclusion of the report was that even in cases where weapons are involved, women can and do successfully resist sexual assault. Women are not always brutally beaten because they resist rape. The study states, *"Women can successfully resist violent rapists even in circumstances where resistance might appear to be futile. Indeed, this study shows that victim resistance is highly correlated with deterrence of sexual assault."*[16]

Although chances for crimes may be greater in some localities at certain times, the differences are often slight. Harassment and assault and rape originate in the man's mind, and where you are is irrelevant. A woman could become a target at any time and in any place. This is not stated to frighten you, but to encourage you to think of your own safety at all times. Like other citizens in today's rapidly changing and often threatening society, you will want to take precautions to insure your safety.

14. Brownmiller, *Against Our Will*, p. 197.
15. Queen's Bench Foundation, *Rape: Prevention and Resistance*, p. 27.
16. Ibid., p. 105.

women and self-defense
2

The economic, social, and psychological roles of women in society are undergoing a profound change. Women are assuming new identities and thinking of themselves in new ways. New freedom and independence are allowing women to pursue their own interests, to go where they wish when they want to go. Unfortunately this freedom has thrust women into a sometimes brutal and hostile world.

Centuries of overprotection, submissiveness, and politeness have provided most women with little experience of thinking in terms of their own protection. Placed in a situation where they are vulnerable and not in control, many women will deny that there is any danger to themselves. Socially conditioned to trust their environment, women have not been trained to look out for dangerous places or people. When something threatening happens, they tend to freeze up inside and reduce their effectiveness in defending themselves.

The average woman is smaller and less muscular than the average man. A woman realizes that relying on her physical strength alone will not defeat a large, strong man. This awareness can be a form of protection; too often it makes her fearful. She will surrender before trying any number of diversions or tactics by which she could escape or overcome her assailant. Before a woman can fully live the newfound life of freedom and independence, she must begin thinking of ways to protect herself against physical and mental assault. If she disregards her personal safety, experiences of rape or assault could become obstacles to her development. She could return to remaining behind locked doors, restrict her activities, and turn inward. No matter how liberated or successful a woman may be, she remains a potential target of violence and crime.

Avoidance of all conflict conditions a person to have a victim's mentality. This can be remedied. One of the greatest changes in the role of women has been in the psychological realm. Although she lacks experience in physical confrontations and fighting, she can learn to protect herself by changing her psychological self-concept.

In a self-defense situation, fear and intimidation are greater handicaps than lack of physical strength or size. A common response to rape is reported in *The Politics of Rape*. "I was so frightened. This wasn't a simple thing of verbal sexist statements being made to me. This was really an attack on me, and I became totally frightened and just froze up. My body went absolutely stiff."[1] The woman, who wasn't facing an armed attacker, gave up before attempting any physical resistance. Such a response can render a woman a totally helpless victim. This experience is common enough to necessitate the development of self-defense consciousness to keep women from surrendering when facing dangers to their health or their mental well-being.

Women can't wait for crime to disappear before they walk the streets and go about their business. The short-term, immediate solution is to develop a self-defense consciousness that will enable a woman to prevent situations from developing into physical altercations. Rather than adjusting to the loss of freedom of movement that crime creates, women are beginning to acquire the skills to cope with many situations they have not faced before.

Attitude changes can affect not only a woman's chances of being preyed upon by criminals but can give her a more positive sense of personal worth. A desire to change and the confidence that she is worthwhile are important factors in learning to change behavior. Coupled with determination to begin seeing herself and her environment in a new way, she can begin to definitively change her behavior to make life safer.[2]

The best form of defense is to anticipate dangerous situations and avoid them. Only after you have taken all realistic precautions and after you have tried to escape will you need physical techniques to defend yourself. Anticipation and escape do not rely upon size, bulk, or fighting skill. Learning self-defense techniques is insurance if you cannot avoid a fight. By changing your psychological attitudes, becoming aware of dangerous situations, and taking reasonable precautions, you will rarely need to use any physical defense skills. The techniques form a foundation that will provide you with psychological and physical security if all else fails.

ALTERNATIVES TO BECOMING A VICTIM

The so-called feminine traits of kindness, compassion, patience, acceptance, and dependence can be exaggerated and contribute to a woman becoming a victim. Inability to say "No" to a stranger, lack of confidence in one's intuition, and inability to express anger and hostility can all play into a criminal's hands. How many times has a trusting woman opened the door to a complete stranger, allowing him to come in and rape her? How often has a woman accepted a ride from several men in a car, although she felt she was being placed in a weak defensive position? How frequently has a woman failed to tell a man she doesn't want to go up to his apartment because she was afraid she might be disliked?

1. Diana E. H. Russell, *The Politics of Rape: The Victim's Perspective* (New York: Stein and Day, 1974), p. 233.

2. Seattle-King County NOW, National Organization of Women, *Woman Assert Yourself! An Instructive Handbook*, (New York: Perennial Library, 1974), p. 21.

Many conscious and unconscious pretenses or "games," where women entice men, can ultimately result in unhappy and destructive experiences. To play a game successfully, the aggressor must get the right message. In a menacing situation a woman cooperates to some extent by not standing up for herself. Rather than terminating the situation before it gets started, she allows it to become an elaborately confused interchange. Such games make a woman appear vulnerable and can encourage a physical attack. The man who is out looking for a woman to victimize senses this behavior and is drawn to her like a magnet. The woman may be so oppressed she does not realize the vulnerable image she projects. The woman who does not insist on being treated as an equal, worthwhile human being is a potential victim for a man intent on rape.[3]

A woman does not have to accept traditional cultural responses. Realizing that sex-role stereotypes incline women to be victims is the first step in beginning to alter one's self-image. An inward change toward a new positive self-image will greatly decrease a woman's vulnerability.

A convincing alternative to becoming a victim is to ask yourself if you are worth fighting for. Make a list of qualities you like about yourself. For what reasons do you consider yourself worth protecting? How strongly do you feel about your self-worth. Is your *self* basically worth defending?

If you consider yourself worth protecting, how much are you willing to assert yourself? What level of response are you capable of when protecting yourself? Suppose you are caught in a situation where you are going to be beaten or murdered. Would you fight back? How much would you be willing to damage a potential attacker if he were a stranger? If he were a friend? How much abuse are you willing to take before you fight back? Are you willing to gouge out an eye to keep from being raped? Beaten? Murdered?

Rather than waiting for a potentially dangerous situation, it is necessary to think beforehand about what you would do and plan your response. How much are you willing to risk? Stop a moment and consider what you are willing to accept from a man threatening aggression against you. What have been your responses in the past? In the light of past experiences would you act the same way? Think of various possibilities in the future and decide what are you willing to do to prevent yourself becoming a victim of harassment and intimidation, murder, robbery, assault, and rape. Of course it is abnormal to fantasize constantly about possible violence. Constantly running fanciful pictures of violence through your mind could cause excessive anxiety and fear. The purpose of this exposition is not to make you worry more but to persuade you to clarify your values and reactions *before* a situation gets out of hand. This will help you to prepare mentally so that you will not be caught off guard and freeze in terror.

Consider realistically the possibility that you could become a victim of an attack. Make a list of past experiences when self-protection was important and opposite them make a column enumerating you responses. Now make a list including intimidation by salesmen, harassment, insults, assault, rape, and

3. Lynn Z. Bloom, Karen Coburn, and Joan Pearlman, *The New Assertive Woman* (New York: Dell-Delacourt Press, 1975), p. 16.

murder. In another column make a note of what risk you would be willing to take to defend yourself. Discuss your responses in class. Are your assessments realistic? What are your goals for this class?

Consider realistically the possibility that you could become a victim of an attack. Make a list of past experiences when self-protection was important, and, opposite to them, make a column enumerating your responses. In retrospect, to what degree do your responses seem appropriate?

Value clarification is important in a preliminary evaluation of your past, present, and future reactions in a variety of self-defense encounters. For example, if you are held up by an armed robber and ordered to hand over your money it would be unwise to fight. Give him the purse. But if you are stopped by an unarmed assailant on the street in a busy neighborhood in the daytime, how would you react? Would you play the poor-little-helpless-me game? If you were grabbed would you react? Would you talk, yell, pull away, counterattack?

Basically, we assume that women taking this course are interested in changing past behavior, are concerned with rising violence, and have a desire to learn to defend themselves. A woman has a right, just like all human beings, to be treated with respect; to have her own opinions, feelings, and desires; to be taken seriously by other people, to decide for herself what is important in life; to be able to say *no*; to turn down another's request or demand without feeling guilty; to make mistakes; and not to be intimidated, harassed, insulted, and made objects of predatory remarks or physical attack.[4] These are personal rights every person is entitled to and which should be respected by others. Unfortunately, they are not always respected. You remain the only one who can insist on your rights; you have to decide whether it is worth your time and energy to see that your rights are respected.

LEARNING TO RECOGNIZE DANGER

In almost every verbal and physical assault there is an initial moment of warning. An assailant will maneuver for position, take an aggressive body posture, or insult you verbally. A stranger may invade personal space by getting too close. A motorist may begin cursing before leaving his car to harass another driver. A leering man in a bar could follow a woman to her car. In most cases a warning sign or indication will give you time to decide what you are going to do before you have to defend yourself physically. Rather than becoming frantic at the first signs of a confrontation, remain as calm as possible. Compose yourself, breathe deeply, and quickly search your surroundings for an escape route or some way to avoid the conflict. Do something out of the ordinary to attract the attention of bystanders, or move to a more crowded area where an attack will be noticed. Sometimes the best

4. Ibid., p. 32-33.

policy is to confront the situation head on and show you are not frightened. If you are going to make a scene and attract attention, an assailant will probably decide it is not worth the risk of being caught.

The more a woman is aware of dangerous people or places, the more she will be able to anticipate harm to herself or her property. Often people become so wrapped up in their immediate activities that they fail to look ahead. When you are driving down the freeway you watch the oncoming traffic. You see the car ahead come to a rolling stop. Knowing you cannot trust the other driver completely, you slow down and are ready to brake. If you watch only the immediate traffic you may fail to observe the other car pulling out in front of you unexpectedly.

Anticipation and foresight are important in many areas of life. The family with a loaded gun in a bedside nightstand and small children can anticipate the possibility of the children finding the gun and accidentally shooting someone. A woman walking alone at night can see a group of men walking toward her and realize they could harm her. Leaving doors unlocked in the city, we can expect that a burglar may eventually find the door open, enter, and rob our apartment.

By referring to newspaper accounts, stories from friends, and past experiences, can you make a list of dangerous situations you are likely to face within the next six months?

Make a list of dangerous situations each of you are likely to face within the next six months. Use newspaper accounts, stories from friends, and past experiences. Attempt for a few minutes to think like a criminal. Do you secure your house or apartment so you will not be burglarized? Do you spend a long time fumbling in your handbag for your car keys when you are in a dark parking lot late at night? Think of ways to protect yourself in these situations. Train your mind in the habit of anticipating danger and begin to reduce the risks you take in your daily life.

Many assaults and murders are the result of family quarrels or arguments between spouses or lovers.[5] These situations are somewhat more difficult to defend against because the victim is related to the man and does not think he will harm her. Sometimes both parties lose control of their anger and emotions. Uncontrollable feelings can take over and the situation can rapidly get out of control. Anger, hostility, and revenge can lead to wife beating and other assaults. Some men will rely on their physical strength to settle an argument.

Try to defuse the situation and calm the other person. Your safety could depend upon keeping arguments from developing into physical confrontations. If you ever fear for your physical safety or life it is best to call for help or to leave. In the long run a marriage counselor or third party can be called in to help negotiate with an angry family member or friend.

5. National Commission on the Causes and Prevention of Violence, *Crimes of Violence*, Vol. 11, pp. 209-10, 216-18.

If you are about to be attacked, is it best to yell "Help me.", "Fire.", or "Rape."? Why should you avoid calling out while struggling with an assailant?

In many cases of reported rape, women had an uneasy foreboding that something bad was about to happen before it happened. The Queen's Bench study in San Francisco found, "When they were asked specifically if they felt suspicious, seventy-five percent of the attempted rape victims said they were suspicious."[6] Although they had trouble identifying the source of their uneasiness, many of the women found a *wrong move* triggered their feelings. Generally the women ignored their suspicions and rationalized their feelings. Rarely did the women consider the possibility of rape. Rather than being embarrassed and dismissing your suspicions, take the safe course and follow your intuitions.

Although there are many myths about female intuition, it is believed we receive messages from body language, and some people probably are more sensitive to these than others. Intuition is defined as direct perceptions of facts or truths independent of any reasoning process. It may come in the form of a feeling or a visualization. One may *sense* what people are going to say, how they are going to move, or that something is going to happen.

You can test your intuition to discover how much you can trust it. During this course make a note of how many times you feel like you can tell what is going to happen next or how a person is going to behave or speak. After you have kept such a list for a week see how many times your intuition matches reality. How much can you trust your intuition? By taking note of your intuition you may be able to avoid situations that are dangerous. As soon as you feel distinctly uncomfortable, you may look for ways to get out of the situation.

It is not enough to test your intuition and anticipate dangerous situations. You have to be willing to act on your perceptions even if they sometimes are wrong. Sometimes you don't have time to prepare. Seizing the *opportunity of the moment* is one of the ways to escape undesirable confrontations. One example would be a woman who stops her car beside a busy highway in the mountains to brush her hair. As she sits with the engine idling, a man approaches the side of the car and points a gun at her. "Unlock the door and scoot over!" the man demands. The woman immediately steps on the gas, speeding away. Another example is a woman being kidnapped and taken to a deserted house. Her kidnapper warns her not to try to get away and leaves the room to go to the bathroom. The woman immediately crawls out a window and escapes. In the first case the woman acts instantly with little forethought. In the second the woman is waiting patiently for an opportunity to escape. The first woman could have been paralyzed by fright and missed her chance to escape. In both cases the women seize the opportunity of the moment because they are alert and fully aware of their surroundings.

6. Queen's Bench Foundation, *Rape*, p. 15.

In most situations nothing can replace your own experience and common sense. Learning to think like a criminal can help you avoid most everyday self-defense situations. You can surmise where a threat will come from and move before it develops.

BEING PARANOID VS. BEING PREPARED

Little has been written in self-defense courses for women regarding the exercise of their basic human rights. Women are urged never to go out without a man to protect them, to inform a neighbor when they leave the house as to how long they will be gone and when they will return, or to wear wigs and carry first aid kits. If these precautions were followed a woman's freedom would be quite restricted.

Too many safety precautions may foster paranoia. Paranoia is "a mental disorder characterized by systematized delusions and the projection of personal conflicts which are ascribed to the supposed hostility from others."[7] In today's world too many people have had unexpected and disastrous experiences for them to be ignored. Everyone has a tendency toward paranoia. When this becomes an obsession, it leads to further fear and terror. The opposite reaction is to say "This couldn't happen to me." Such a conclusion is a denial of reality. Reviewing the statistics and the experiences of friends makes us realize we could become the victim of a crime. This can form the basis for a rational process of recognizing the need to be prepared in the event we are threatened.

An exaggerated reaction could be to watch suspiciously every man on the street, thinking he may be the one who will attack. Fear lies behind this response, and a criminal could sense the woman's consternation and attack her. The alternative to this irrational response, with its inherent dread, is to recognize the possibilities of crime and to train ourselves mentally and physically to cope with such a situation. You may find that becoming aware of dangerous situations makes you more afraid during the first few weeks of class. This is a normal reaction. Doctors in medical schools, for example, often develop symptoms of the diseases they are studying. Because they have never noticed certain characteristics of their own bodies, they think they may be abnormal. But as they study more, they are able accurately to diagnose the disease. You are probably developing your feelings of fear out of wonder at your past innocence. Some students may drop the course at this point. You must realize others have the same feelings and that fear is a distinctive instinct. Although no amount of training in physical self-defense will eliminate fear, training will help you channel this instinctual fear into a definite course of action. When you are threatened, you will be better prepared to respond physically.

7. *The American College Dictionary*, (New York Random House, 1962), p. 879.

LEARNING ASSERTIVENESS

The man who molests, intimidates, or attacks a woman usually relies on creating terror, catching the woman off guard, and rendering her compliant.[8] Anything a woman can do to disrupt his game may obstruct and impede his attempt. By responding as a conscious, rational person and remaining as calm as possible, you can neutralize and counteract the sudden attack. By taking psychological control of a situation you can greatly increase the possibilities of escaping harm. Being in control of yourself and your emotions and having self-assurance can help you to assume control. But to be useful in an emergency, self-assurance and control must become part of your daily life.

Submissive behavior is self-perpetuating, and the cycle must be broken in order to reverse the process. Being passive and at the mercy of another makes a person feel bad and helpless about herself. This leads to fear or anger. The more depressed we feel, the more anxious we become in anticipating events that will harm us. Loss of self-confidence and self-esteem lead to anxiety, which in turn leads to further compliant behavior. Eventually the habits of submissive behavior become permanent.

By following the exercises in this section you can begin to focus on changing your behavior in a protected environment so that you will gradually be able to gain more self-confidence and face menacing situations in new ways. When you begin to assert yourself with confidence, you will get results. Anxiety will lessen and you will be able to clarify your own rights, wishes, and desires. As others see you act in new ways they will treat you differently and this will further reinforce your behavior, enabling you to become a more complete and dynamic person.

Changes are not without some disadvantages. Your friends may be accustomed to your doing what they want, never saying "No" to their requests. They may feel threatened with your new self-esteem and self-directedness. Sometimes it may not seem worth the trouble to assert yourself; some issues may be too trivial. Don't be discouraged, but work steadily in pursuit of your own goals. In the long run your friends will respect you more.

One method of beginning to assert yourself is role playing. Role playing is acting out a situation by playing the various roles involved. You can play the role of a man harassing a woman, and you can play the woman's role. Assuming you are the antagonist will enable you to anticipate what he will say and do. You will gain insights into how an antagonist will act toward you. This procedure can help reduce your anxiety and provide you with the confidence and courage to face the real situation if and when it occurs. Try to play your role and not be self-conscious. Pretend you are an actor in a play and attempt to play your role.

---

8. Brownmiller, *Against Our Wills*, p. 385.

EXERCISE

Break up into pairs and have each person take turns playing the man's and the woman's roles. The most important consideration is whether your response is going to be: (1) you want to keep the friendship, (2) you never want to see the other person again, or (3) you are undecided and want to play it extemporaneously. The person playing the man's role should be persistent and give the woman a difficult time. The woman should not tell the man which response she has chosen until after the exercise.

1. The scene is a bar. The man wants to walk the woman home. She has met him before and doesn't want him to. The man persists, asking questions like "What's wrong with me?" "You know how unsafe the streets are.", and "Why are you so uptight?"
2. Your boss wants you to accompany him on a business trip. You have only worked at the place a short time and don't know if you can trust him. You don't want to go. How do you handle the situation?
3. You are walking down the street and two men about your size stop you. They want you to come up to their apartment with them. You aren't going. You are also afraid they may try to harm you on the street.

Check with your partner and see if your intentions were clear about accepting or rejecting the suggestions. Did you continue the relationship in each of these cases? Are your answers clear or are you giving a double message? Did you feel comfortable in each situation? Did you feel the outcome was appropriate? Does either of you have any suggestions on how to get your messages across better?

Analyze your exercises in a different way. Does your behavior fall in the aggressive, submissive, or assertive category? What about your everyday behavior?

Aggressive behavior often builds up because of anger, hostility, and self-righteousness. Expressing needs, feelings, and ideas at the expense of others characterizes aggressive behavior. Ignoring, dominating, or humiliating others are all forms of hostile defensive aggression. Sometimes aggression is aroused by ignoring or being insensitive to another's behavior. At times it is used as a form of intimidation to get something you want.[9]

Assertive behavior is when you stand up for yourself; in this context it should not violate the rights of others. To be assertive indicates that the woman feels good about herself. She is honest, direct, expressive, self-enhancing, and straightforward. Usually she will be an independent, self-motivated person.[10]

Behavior is seldom consistent. More often a person's behavior vacilates from one extreme to another. One cause of this is not expressing one's feeling but rather being submissive. Resentment toward others builds up, the person becomes anxious, and will lose control at any time. The outburst of anger or tears may appear irrelevant to the original issue.

9. Bloom, Coburn, and Pearlman, *The New Assertive Woman*, p. 18.
10. Ibid., p. 18-19.

You have the right to not assert yourself. You also have the option of deciding to be aggressive and to defy or denounce a person. In either case you should be aware of the choices open to you. Making decisions consciously and afterwards being satisfied with them will allow you to retain your confidence and self-respect.

EXERCISE

In the following exercises assume the roles you had in the preceding exercise. This time when you play the role of the woman (yourself), attempt to display assertive behavior. Will you answer a request or demand in an assertive manner? Will you feel comfortable?

1. A man you only recently met and don't know very well wants you to go to a movie with him. You have seen him in class eyeing other women and are suspicious of his intentions. How do you say no?
2. A stranger stops you on the street and asks for directions. You answer only because you are familiar with the store he asks for. But he doesn't want to leave. He wants you to go to a bar and have a drink with him. You have planned on going to a restaurant alone.
3. A man you have been dating wants greater sexual intimacy with you. How do you say no without being aggressive or submissive? Can you retain the friendship? Are you fearful if you say no he won't see you again?

Discuss your responses with your partner and see if your messages have been assertive. Does either of you have any suggestions to make to the other? Has your message gotten across clearly and precisely? Discuss your experiences with the class. Do you have any further insights?

One reason for confusion in the communication is the vague, ambivalent nature of body language. Yet body language accounts for well over half of our communication; most of such language is subconscious.[11] We seldom get a chance to see ourselves as others see us and may not realize we are giving signals that are not clear. Nonverbal, or body, language includes facial expressions, posture, gestures, tone of voice, mannerisms, body movements, giggling, laughter, and many more things. Much of our verbal communication can be reduced or exaggerated by the way we speak, gesture, and stand.[12] For example, a woman is stopped on the street by a man. She wants to leave but is afraid to antagonize the man; there are other people walking on the street and stores nearby. The woman may say something very assertive like, "Leave me alone. I don't want to talk to you." At the same time the woman may be standing with her eyes downcast, her shoulders hunched, her hands clasped tightly in front of her, and her voice a mere squeak. Her verbal message is quite clear, but she belies her true feelings of fear by submissive, nonverbal body language. The man hears what she says, but her actions speak much

11. Albert E. Scheflen, M.D., *Body Language and Social Order* (Englewood Cliffs, N.J.: Prentice-Hall, 1972), p. xii.

12. Bloom, Coburn, and Pearlman, *The New Assertive Woman*, p. 147.

louder than her words. He knows she is afraid and possibly won't put up a fight if he drags her into an alley.

The woman could set her face in hard lines, place her hand on her hip, and glare back at the man while tapping her foot on the sidewalk. She could repeat the same words, sticking her chin forward and waving her arm. Her anger and hostility speak louder than her words. Depending upon the determination of the assailant, her aggressive behavior could involve her in a physical confrontation.

An assertive response is expressed when the woman is self-assured, confident, and projects a strong image. She maintains eye contact. By standing straight and speaking in a commanding voice as if she expects to be taken seriously, she conveys her message and makes the same point much more clearly. It is probable that this woman will be left alone.

EXERCISE

Break up into groups of eight or ten people. Form a U shape, spacing yourselves an arm's length apart. One person at a time should walk through the open end of the U, looking at each person as she goes by. Turn around and walk out of the group. How did you feel? How does the group feel you are conveying your presence through body language?

Next walk into the group in a submissive way, like a wilting flower. Try it again in an aggressive manner as though you are threatening the group by your presence. Third, try to walk into the U in an assertive manner, as if you are self-confident and able to take care of yourself. You want neither to be too timid nor too belligerent. For variety have each person walk into the group and have the group attempt to guess which body language is being displayed. Which image do you project most of the time? Do you feel comfortable with that image? Is it you? Attempt to recall this assertive image you project with your body language as you practice during the course.

In any situation where you need to defend yourself it is important to keep talking in an assertive manner. This will help prevent you from freezing up in fear, make the attacker realize you are a living human being, and will provide more information about what the attacker wants. Combined with assertive body language and an assertive voice, you let the attacker know you are not going to roll over and play dead. In many cases this will be enough to discourage an attack.

When you need to use physical techniques for your defense, they can be combined with your voice to help take the attacker by surprise and aid you in gaining control. Many women will scream in terror when faced with physical attack. A scream is a sound of hopelessness arising from pain or panic. If people are nearby they can be frightened away by fear. Rather than screaming, you will want your voice to become a forceful weapon in your defense. You should therefore yell before you are attacked, when you are counterattacking, or when you are running away. Yelling when grappling with an attacker may lead him to strangle you to stop your yelling. A cry will more likely bring people to your rescue if it sounds as though you are holding your own. Using a yell with a release from a hold or with a powerful counterattack can take an assailant by surprise and stun him.

A yell should be loud, sharp, penetrating, and clear. To yell properly force air up from the center of your body with your diaphragm and abdominal muscles. Take a deep breath and shout on the exhale. Focus the yell at your assailant as if it were a physical weapon. You may not have time for deep breaths when you are in an emergency, but if you do it will help release tension and anxiety. The yell can serve as a catalyst stimulating your mind and body to more powerful action.

EXERCISE

Pair off with a partner. Have one person walk along in a straight line toward the other. The second person should stop the first and shove her forcefully from the front. The first person should stop, take a deep breath, and yell forcefully from the abdominal cavity. Try to feel the air come up from the center of your body. Focus your attention totally on the other person when you yell. Shout "no," "hey," "fire," or a single syllable. In the past, yelling rape has not proved successful in bringing assistance. "Fire," on the other hand, affects many people and could lead to property damage, so that others are less likely to ignore it.

Next, let one partner walk and let the second partner push from any direction. Turn immediately to face the second person, halt, and yell. Try to overcome any inhibition or self-consciousness by letting the yell come from deep within. Does it express your willpower? Would an assailant be frightened? Is your yell loud enough for others to hear if they are nearby? Repeat this exercise until you become relaxed. Use the yell when counterattacking. Make it part of your arsenal when moving against an assailant.

The greater your defense consciousness and your ability to recognize danger, the better prepared you will be for making a quick decision in a threatening situation. *The physical techniques you learn in this course can never replace your judgment in avoiding danger.* The best personal defense is always to avoid danger, find an escape route, or neutralize the situation. Your self-defense skills can increase the distance between you and your attackers, thus greatly improving your chances of escape.

training basics

3

Mastering the physical principles of self-defense requires practicing the moves until they become part of subconscious reflex action. Many physical attacks are a complete surprise, planned to catch a woman unaware and off balance. They are a form of terrorism designed to instill fear in the victim and break down resistance. When self-defense techniques become an intuitive response, they can throw an attacker off balance and allow you to escape.

Fear of serious injury or death is the reason most often cited for compliance in a rape or mugging. A physical reaction of tightening the thorax and constricting breathing, stiffening muscles, and paralysis accompany fear. A correct subconscious response, however, can immediately set the body in motion eliminating fear at its source and providing a calm foundation for preventive action.

Attacks can be deterred by a rapid response. Those who have successfully escaped rape attempts are more assertive physically, and they employ more resistance methods in an attack than do rape victims.[1] Rapists are afraid of being caught and will often desist if they encounter strong resistance. But don't count on it! Never underestimate an attacker! You have no way to tell what is in his mind.

Complex or complicated moves are not easily recollected in an emergency, but simple, direct techniques can be recalled easily and remembered for years. They can be reviewed often to remind your body of proper responses and such review increases their effectiveness. A short-course in self-defense will not provide you with the skills for a long, drawn-out fight against a larger, stronger, and more powerful assailant. It can, however, increase your self-confidence and provide you with many techniques with which to escape an attack.

1. Queen's Bench Foundation, Rape, p. 19.

RELAXATION

Total mobilization of the body in an emergency can elicit superhuman feats of strength. Fear and tension, on the other hand, dissipate strength. Then the muscles of the bronchial tube tighten, making breathing shorter and shallower. Excessive muscular tension causes the muscles to freeze, limiting fluidity and range of motion, while prolonged tension leads to fatigue. Moreover, anxiety impairs thinking and disrupts coordination, increasing susceptibility to injury.

Test your ability to relax consciously by lying supine on the floor. Release as much tension as possible before having a partner lift your forearm from the floor and then let it drop. Did your arm fall limply as a dead weight or remain suspended?

One important objective in self-defense is to learn how to relax so that mental tension will not dissipate your physical strength. Often removing the physiological manifestations of an emotion will eliminate the expression of emotion. If you do not already practice a relaxation technique, you probably find yourself getting tense even during practice sessions. Pause and breathe deeply, being aware of breathing through your nose and absorbing the breath into your center. Hold the breath for a few moments and slowly exhale. If you still have trouble because you are tense and anxious, lie down on the floor and consciously tense all of your muscles lifting your head, arms, and legs off the floor in total tension (fig. 3.1). Suddenly let the tension go and let your limbs fall to the floor (fig. 3.2). By perceiving the difference between total relaxation and total tension, relaxation will come easier. Relaxation allows your body to move flexibly, fluidly, and quickly. Rather than becoming like the unyielding oak tree, which comes crashing to earth in a strong wind, become like the flexible willow tree, which successfully resists the pressure of the wind by bending freely.

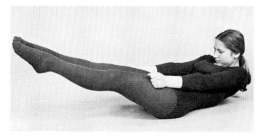

Fig. 3.1   Fig. 3.2

PROJECTION

Our bodies are composed of muscles, bones, joints, and ligaments, but our bodies also contain an energy that can be directed by our minds. In acupuncture, *tai chi*, and Chinese medicine, this power is known as *chi*, the life-force energy that fills our bodies. In aikido and karate it is called *ki*. While there is no direct English translation, such words as willpower, mental power, and life force describe this force. We choose to call this energy *dynamic willpower* to emphasize that it is controlled by our conscious and subconscious mind. This power is real and has physical effects. You can cultivate this power so that it will grow and become stronger.

Just as a karate blow strikes *through* a board, our dynamic willpower can project beyond our physical bodies to add greater power to our movements. A simple experiment will illustrate this principle in a direct and measurable way. Face a partner. Rest your wrist on her shoulder. Clench your fist and tense the muscles of your arm. Let your partner push down on your elbow with both hands, testing the strength of your muscle power (fig. 3.3). Your partner may not immediately be able to bend your arm, but you will require a great deal of strength to keep your arm straight.

Relax your arm by shaking your hand as though you were slinging water off your finger tips. Let your arm dangle at your side in a relaxed and natural position. Slowly raise your arm keeping the same conformation it had when it was at your side. Your arm will be slightly bent and your fingers extended. Imagine your body filling with energy flowing from the center of your hips and running along the bottom of your arm. Imagine a powerful stream of water or electricity flowing from your outstretched fingers. Rest your hand on your partner's shoulder and project your energy toward the horizon as if it were a beam. Concentrate on keeping your shoulders relaxed. Continue to exert this energy when your partner presses down on your arm (fig. 3.4). Keep your balance. Let your partner repeat the exercise.

Your partner will have a much more difficult time bending your arm when you use your muscular power. This exercise illustrates the power of your mind, which we call projection. As you practice the techniques described in this book, your ability to focus this energy will slowly increase.

Fig. 3.3   Fig. 3.4

BALANCE

When at rest, our balance is several inches below the navel, centered between the hips. As we move, our bodies function in a natural, coordinated way to maintain our balance in an upright position. When confronted with a new activity, the body compensates until balance is reacquired for the new activity. Balance is the point at which the forces acting on your body are zero. If you are off balance, your muscles must do extra work to keep your body from falling over. You will need to balance and coordinate your strength.

Body balance is generally maintained at the hips, where the mass of your body is concentrated. By upsetting a taller, stronger, and heavier attacker's balance and maintaining your own, you can minimize his strength and maximize your own. The hips contain the strongest muscles in the body. These muscles, used in conjunction with balance and projection, enable you to multiply the muscle power of your arms and legs many times. To illustrate, have a partner face you and grip your hands with his (fig. 3.5). Step straight back, pulling against the grip with your arm muscles (fig. 3.6). Nothing happens unless you are much stronger. Next, keeping both arms relaxed, step straight back maintaining your normal posture. Move from your hips first, keeping your balance, and your partner will naturally follow (fig. 3.7). Practice a few times until you become accustomed to moving your center of balance. Combine this action with twisting the side of your wrist against the thumb of the hand that is holding yours; this is an effective technique to use against being grabbed or pulled (fig. 3.8a) (closeup, 3.8b).

The most efficient self-defense techniques are designed to initially upset the balance of an attacker, while avoiding direct confrontation with his power. Maintain your own balance throughout each technique. To double check yourself, stop the movement at the point you suspect you may be off balance. Freeze your position and let your partner step aside. If you are

Fig. 3.5   Fig. 3.6

Fig. 3.7

Fig. 3.8a

Fig. 3.8b

properly maintaining your balance your hips will be beneath you, your shoulders will both be down and relaxed, and the position will feel natural and comfortable.

Your head plays an important part in maintaining balance. Looking down or to one side can throw your balance off. Especially in the beginning, your eyes and head will direct and help project your dynamic willpower. Greater physical strength can be manifested by coordinating your head, torso, and hips. Your hands, arms, and legs will become appendages radiating out from the center of your hips. When you throw a partner, look in the direction you plan to throw. Looking back at an attacker will present your face as an inviting target and will tend to throw you off balance and reduce your power. The force of your mind together with coordinated body balance will put you in the strongest possible position.

EXERCISES

Developing a self-defense attitude and projecting a positive self-image under stress requires using the whole body and mind in a coordinated way. Self-defense responses that are part of the subconscious mind are more fluid and can be employed without time-consuming thought. The process of fusing mind and body can begin with warm-up exercises.

The following exercises are designed to apply specific principles of self-defense during the initial warm-ups. While the standard jumping jack is a good cardiovascular exerise, it will not help when you are directly confronted with a self-defense situation. Thus, other exercises are useful. Push-ups give tone to the muscles and develop strength in the biceps. Being in good physical condition will help you indirectly when you need to defend yourself, but the specific warm-up exercises presented here combine relaxation, projection of your mental will power, and keeping balance while in motion; they increase flexibility, dexterity, and agility.

Learning to move the body as one unit means coordinating torso, hips, legs, and arms, while projecting your dynamic willpower outward. This will do more to increase your total power than will developing muscular strength. Developing strength alone often means relying upon that strength rather than concentrating on coordinating the power one already possesses. Essentially it doesn't make sense for a smaller, lighter, and weaker person to attempt to build powerful muscles for the purpose of meeting an attacker's force head on.

When performing the exercises, be alert and aware of your body. If practiced daily for ten to fifteen minutes, the exercises will prepare you for the classes, increasing your blood circulation and cardiovascular efficiency. Do more than a routine one-two-three-four body-bend. Fill your body with your dynamic willpower, breath deeply, and focus your attention on the muscles being stretched. When bending, be aware of your energy flowing out of your finger tips beyond your physical body. When standing or sitting be aware of the point at which your body balances as you shift from one exercise to another. Retain your balance while moving as well as in static positions.

Flexibility is not increased when the body is cold. These exercises are designed to relax the body in a systematic fashion before practicing the techniques. Once a week, at the end of class, repeat the exercises, stretching further to increase flexibility. Are you gradually becoming more limber?

A WORD OF CAUTION: Stretch each muscle to its limit in a smooth and continuous motion, being careful not to jerk, bounce or overstretch. Let the mind relax and the motions become effortless. At first you may not be able to bend very far. That's okay—don't hurry, take your time working into the stretch gradually during the course. It may take a long period of time before you become looser and more flexible. Alternate stretching on each side, breathing deeply as you reach the limits of your stretch. Remember these exercises are to relax your body more than to increase your range of motion. Relaxation will protect you from muscle pulls.

Torso-Leg Stretches

1. Sit on the floor with your legs together, outstretched in front of you. Point your toes back toward your body. Bend from the waist to touch your head to your knees. Keep your knees straight for a good stretch along the back of the legs. Project your mind forward toward your toes (fig. 3.9).
2. Stretch both legs away from your body as far as possible. At first your toes will flatten out, pointing away from your body. With practice you will be able to curl your toes and keep them pointing upward. Reach overhead with the opposite hand and stretch toward the knee. With time, you will be able to move the legs outward stretching them farther apart before bending to the knees (fig. 3.10).

Fig. 3.9

Fig. 3.10

Fig. 3.11

Fig. 3.12   Fig. 3.13

3. Bend at the waist, attempting to keep the back straight as you try to touch your forehead to the mat in front of you (fig. 3.11).
4. Sitting upright with your back straight, bring the soles of the feet together. Rock both knees up and down, attempting to touch the knees to the mat. Next bend the body downward, keeping the back straight, attempting to touch your head to the mat or the toes (fig. 3.12).
5. With your legs together in front of you swing them over your head touching your toes behind you on the mat. Hold for five seconds. Come forward and bend your head to your knees for five seconds. Repeat four times (fig. 3.13).

Ankles

With one leg straight out in front of you, bring the opposite calf to your thigh, grasping above the ankle with one hand. Grasp the toes with the other hand and rotate the ankle in full circles in both directions ten times each. Hold the toes and grasp the foot, bringing the toes forward and backward as far as they will go. Raise the foot off the thigh and let the foot relax as you shake the ankle.

Torso Stretch

1. Standing, spread both feet a little wider than shoulder width. Bend forward at the waist and touch your hands behind you between your legs. Reach overhead with both hands, exhaling as you bend to the rear as far as possible. Repeat four times (fig. 3.14).
2. With a natural curve in your arm, reach one hand above your head, thumb down and palm facing away from your body. Let the other hand slide down your leg as you bend from the waist. Let the energy flow along the little finger side of your arm, which is curving over your head toward the mat. Repeat five times slowly on each side (fig. 3.15).

Fig. 3.14   Fig. 3.15

Shoulders

1. Let your waist become flexible as you rotate it first to one side and then the other in a smooth, continuous motion. Let your arms relax and be carried along by the force of your hips rotating. Let the balls of your feet turn slightly with the motion. Repeat ten times (fig. 3.16).
2. Begin with your arms outstretched above your head. Rotate from the hips, letting your arms make a full circle down toward the mat, then up above and behind your head. Keep your eyes forward and retain your balance. Repeat ten times.

Neck Stretches

Bring both feet to shoulder width. Rotate the head slowly, looking up as far as possible. Bring the chin slowly to the chest. Stretch to the full limits of your neck motion. Next, move the head straight up and down and look slowly to the left and right as far as possible. Then tilt the head, moving the right ear to the right shoulder and repeat on the left. Adjusting your center of gravity in your abdomen and keeping your attention and eyes forward, rotate the neck in full circles. Repeat five times each way.

Wrist

Relaxing the shoulders let both hands fall to your sides. Shake your hands vigorously, letting the hands swing freely as if you were flinging water from the tips of your fingers. Shake fifteen to twenty times. After you stop you will feel a tingling sensation in your hands. Your shoulders will be relaxed. Although you are very relaxed your hands will feel very *alive*. Try to keep this feeling as you practice.

Leg Stretch

Standing, spread both legs wider than shoulder width. Bend your right knee and lower your body toward the floor. Attempt to keep your right heel on the floor as your upper body turns slightly toward the left. Let the left foot come up onto the heel with the toes pointed up and your left knee straight as you lower your body. Use your hands on the mat in front of you to shift back and fourth from left to right, getting a good stretch in your legs. For an added stretch, attempt to bend your forehead to the outstretched knee. Repeat six times (fig. 3.17).

Waist Stretch

Bring both feet together. Place your hands on your hips and make large circles with your hips. Make ten circles each way.

Relaxing the Whole Body

Relax your body and bring your hands to your sides, allowing them to hang naturally. Spread your feet slightly apart. Spring into the air with the power coming from the toes and keeping the knees slightly bent. Repeat ten times.

Fig. 3.16   Fig. 3.17

developing
self-defense
reactions
4

BASIC STANCE

A defensive posture involves a stance in which a person is squared off and ready to fight. It implies a challenge and could unintentionally invite an attack. Because surprise is often an important element in your favor, you need to assume a natural, comfortable position from which you can move quickly and strongly. An effective stance is an erect, relaxed posture, with your head forward and your attention focused on the attacker. Your feet should be approximately shoulder width apart, with the forward foot pointed directly at the attacker and the rear foot turned out at a 45- to-90-degree angle. Your heels should be approximately on a straight line. Weight is evenly distributed on both feet, while shoulders and hips are slightly rotated. The leading shoulder is the same as the forward foot (fig. 4.1). This slight rotation presents less of your body as a target.

Looking your attacker straight in the eyes can be distracting. Although some people claim a person looks at the target before he or she punches or grabs, such an assumption could be dangerous. Fighters may also feint with their eyes to throw their opponent off balance. Do not focus your attention on any particular spot. Look beyond the attacker so he becomes part of the overall view. Concentrate your attention looking forward, but do not let your head bend forward. Gazing in this manner will help make an encounter less personal. It will allow you to compose yourself without being caught up in the emotions of fear or feelings of sympathy for the intentions of an attacker. Taking in the whole body with your gaze will enable you in an instant to see the movement of the body, the hands, or the feet.

The basic stance provides a protected position. Assume your stance and extend both hands in front of you until the finger tips touch. You will notice your body presents a triangle (fig. 4.2). As you practice, attempt to keep the point of the triangle aimed at your partner. Turning the point away will present your side as a target. This stance can be crucial in emergencies and promotes a good, erect posture. It is never unbalanced. Rather than slouching

Fig. 4.1   Fig. 4.2

against a wall or standing with one leg dangling around the other, practice this posture as you wait in a line or talk to friends. With your *dynamic will-power* flowing forward, your balance in your hips and your knees relaxed, the basic stance is less tiring, less threatening, and always serves as a point of departure in an emergency.

APPROPRIATE DISTANCE

Always maintain appropriate distance from a potential attacker. If someone attempts to stop you on the street move to one side, out of reach. Keep walking while verbally asserting your decision. If a suspicious group of men is on your side of the street, cross to the other side of the street long before you get to them. When confronted or cornered in a building, be alert and aware of escape routes or obstructions you can use. Any object that can be placed between you and an assailant to keep him from grabbing or striking you should be used. Obstructions can give you time to yell for help, to plan an escape route, or to distract the attacker's attention. Try to use an obstruction large enough to present a real barrier, like a desk or table if you are indoors, or a hedge or bench if outside. Objects like lamps, chairs, or tables can be overturned in an attacker's path. Upset these objects or throw them at the knees of an attacker. Don't let them become weapons to be used against you. Keep the obstruction in front of you, stay low, mobile, agile, and move fast. If an attacker leaps at you, throwing himself off balance, that may be your chance to counterattack or flee.

In any confrontation there is a maneuvering for position. One of the most important aspects of this maneuvering is staying out of reach. Crucial distance is the margin of safety you have when facing an assailant. As the distance is decreased your assailant comes closer to you, and it becomes increasingly difficult to defend yourself against sudden movements. Increase the distance, and your assailant must take several steps to reach you.

From your basic stance facing a partner with your forward arms extended, your fingertips should almost meet (fig. 4.3). You should stay just beyond this distance so that an assailant will have to take a step forward in order to reach you (fig. 4.4). If your assailant inches forward, don't let yourself be hemmed in. Step back at a 45 degree angle or circle to the side. Alert your arm muscles, but keep them relaxed. If your assailant lunges, raise your hands with your elbows protecting your sides and thrust the outside edges of your hands forward with your finger tips pointing up (fig. 4.5).

Pair off with a partner and practice maintaining this crucial distance, facing with first one foot forward and then the other. The distance will vary depending upon the height and reach of individual partners. Maintain the awareness of crucial distance and develop it so that it becomes second nature or habitual. Many women who have been attacked have sensed the threat before they were attacked. If you can't get away, keep the crucial distance. By relaxing and having the proper balance and spacing you should have sufficient time to move before an attacker reaches you.

PIVOTING AND CHANGING DIRECTION

The basic stance provides a base from which you can move quickly and decisively. A stationary target can be quickly reached. Proper distancing forces an attacker to take a step forward to reach you. This gives you time to pivot

---

Have you practiced the basic pivot until you can make a speedy and accurate quarter or half turn to the left and right and with either foot forward?

Fig. 4.3   Fig. 4.4   Fig. 4.5

and get out of the way or to change directions in order to take advantage of an obstacle or an escape route.

A simple pivot can put you out of an attacker's reach. From the basic stance with either foot pointing forward, look straight ahead, extending your right hand at waist level (fig. 4.6). Shift your balance slightly to the balls of your feet, keeping your weight evenly distributed and your balance intact. You are going to turn 180 degrees so you will be looking in the opposite direction. Lines on the floor or mat will help. Your weight shifts to the ball of your forward foot and you begin the pivot, moving your head first to look in the opposite direction and bring your right hand to your center (fig. 4.7). Your hips are turned powerfully, swinging your rear foot all the way around so you face in the opposite direction, extending both hands in front of your body (fig. 4.8). You will observe, if you practice on a straight line, that your body begins to turn on one side of the line and completes the movement on the opposite side of the line. This exercise is particularly helpful in learning to maintain your balance while in motion.

The basic pivot allows you to turn in any segment of a circle. Pivoting is the surest way to retain balance and move through the shortest arc in the least time. It is also useful in running away. If you begin running and an attacker chases, you will be able to judge how close he is by the noises he makes. Turning your head to see where he is will slow you down and throw you off balance. While running is the best defense in many situations, it will not guarantee your safety. If you are attacked in a lonely place and are able to pivot free you will want to counterattack so that your attacker won't jump on your back as you turn to flee. Deciding to run depends on the situation, but once you have decided on a course of action, don't hesitate. Take short determined steps, leaning forward at a 10 degree angle for a fast take-off. With your arms flexed at a 90 degree angle, bring them up so that your upper arm is parallel to the ground. Use your arms to propel your body forward. Don't let your arms wave about and waste motion. Come down on

Fig. 4.6   Fig. 4.7   Fig. 4.8

the balls of your feet initially. Only when you are out of danger is it safe to shift to the heel-toe gait with your body in a more upright, jogging position.

For Added Practice

Go outside and repeat the pivoting exercise, with the addition of running. Have your partner chase you. Use the surprise of an initial pivot, and see whether you can outrun your partner. Next, let your partner come close enough to reach out and touch you, then suddenly pivot. You may want to feint to one side and run in the opposite direction. Be sure your turns are timed correctly so your partner can't cut you off at a corner. As you change direction, pivot on the foot farthest from your partner and push off in the new direction forcefully. Becoming familiar with the pivot will greatly increase your ability to keep your balance and serve as a basis in many of the following techniques.

BLENDING

Stopping to oppose or halt an onrushing attacker is foolish. Only if you are much stronger and heavier than he would you hope to stop him head on. By taking advantage of an attack and redirecting the attack, you do not confront power with power. An initial example will illustrate the strategy and help you to understand the principles. Face your partner, both of you with opposite foot and hand forward, your partner grasping your outstretched hand in a firm grip (fig. 4.9). His strength is exerted by his arm stretched toward you. If you stiffen your elbow and shoulder and try to move forward or pull back you can't move. The movements are similar to the pivot. You should take advantage of the force he is applying to your wrist. (Actually, you should never let an assailant grab hold of you; if you can't move fast enough, you can still move.) Bend the hand that is being held at the wrist so that your fingers point back toward yourself. Your strength should be exerted in the same direction as that toward which your partner's force is being applied. Slide your front foot forward four or five inches and bring your hips toward your own hand, maintaining the projection in the hand that is being held (fig. 4.10). Pivot suddenly on the ball of the forward foot, letting your rear foot move around to the rear. As you make the pivot, look in the direction you plan to turn; this will help your body to turn naturally. Your elbow and shoulder should be relaxed; if not, they will lock and prevent you from turning. After turning, keep your hips slightly forward so your knee forms a straight line with your forward toe. Your partner will be pulled slightly off balance (fig. 4.11) Practice this until you can do it while keeping your balance and stability.

Most of the techniques in this course are based on blending, where your motion smoothly joins the motion of your partner rather than opposing it in a direct confrontation. If you feel yourself using a great deal of force to oppose your partner, or if she is stopping you, something is wrong. It may be necessary to relax your grip until your partner can perform the movement correctly. In general you want to use an attacker's force as much as possible, and take advantage of his move in such a way as to leave him vulnerable to a counterattack and elude him, using a grab, kick, or punch.

ENTERING

One of the greatest advantages of being relaxed during a confrontation is your ability to react swiftly. This does not mean that your body is limp, but rather that it is relaxed with a living, positive feeling generated by your concentration and determination. Once you are relaxed, you will be able to observe any move an attacker makes and react swiftly. If you know you are in a dangerous situation, you may be able to take advantage of the attacker's force on his blind, unprotected side.

Stand facing your partner with the same hand and same foot forward. Check for proper distancing. Let your partner step forward to grasp your forward hand with his other hand (fig. 4.12). If you are calm you will be able to anticipate his move before it reaches you. Just as his hand begins to touch your wrist, move your forward foot ahead, taking a deep sliding step behind him. Let your rear foot follow so you face in the same direction behind his outstretched hand (fig. 4.13). Let the arm your partner is grasping for bend limply at the elbow, moving it toward your stomach. Come down with your opposite hand as you glide by behind his hand (fig. 4.14). Be sure the attack is committed before you move. If you move too slowly you will be caught and if you move too soon your partner can simply follow you. Check your balance to see if your posture is erect, your weight evenly distributed on both feet, and your balance stable. Your feet should be shoulder-width apart.

As you stand facing an attacker, there is nothing to indicate what he will do. He may punch, lunge to grasp your body, or attempt to choke you. It does not matter which hand he grabs with or from which side he lunges.

Fig. 4.9   Fig. 4.10   Fig. 4.11

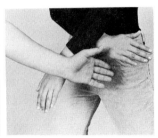

Fig. 4.12   Fig. 4.13   Fig. 4.14

Every attack by its very nature leaves the attacker with a vulnerable spot, a weakness you can learn to exploit (figs. 4.15a, 4.15b). Entering and taking advantage of his move can provide time to follow up with a counterattack, to use an obstruction, for someone to intervene, or it can give you added time to find an escape route. Persuade an attacker that you will not meekly surrender. These exercises demonstrate the underlying principles of body movement, balance, posture, and using your mind and body as a whole.

FALLING

In order to maximize your strength you need mobility, speed, and timing. This means staying on your feet. The basic exercises will help you maintain balance while in motion. But what happens if you lose your footing or are thrown to the ground? Your best defense is to rise immediately. Try to make

Fig. 4.15a   Fig. 4.15b

a fall smooth and painless, to help you in any situation where you lose your balance and fall, whether it be on an icy sidewalk or on a dark road.

When you think of taking a fall from a standing position the floor will appear very distant. You can lower your body swiftly so as to make a long fall a short one. Lower your body in stages, attempting to make the fall as smooth and rounded as possible. The simplest fall is a back roll. Stand in your basic position, with your right foot forward. Lift your left foot and place it behind you with the tops of your toes on the mat (fig. 4.16) Bend both legs at the knees and slowly lower yourself onto your left knee (fig. 4.17). Shifting your weight to the rear, sit down on your heel and roll back with your chin tucked in (fig. 4.18). Roll back onto your left shoulder (fig. 4.19a). Rock forward and rise in the same sequence in which you went down (fig. 4.19b). Keep your mind and gaze focused forward. Avoid crossing your ankles which will prevent you from rising (fig. 4.20). When you rise, you should be in a balanced ready posture and able to move swiftly.

If you get dizzy practicing rolls or have trouble relaxing, exhale as you roll and make the roll as quiet as possible. For additional practice, stand facing forward and have your partner push you suddenly on one shoulder or the

Fig. 4.16

Fig. 4.17

Fig. 4.18

Fig. 4.19a

Fig. 4.19b

Fig. 4.20

other. Take the roll on the shoulder opposite of that which your partner pushes. As you rise to your feet pivot to face your partner. After this is accomplished, let your partner lunge at you. As he lunges repeat the initial motion described above. Knowing how to roll will minimize injury if you are thrown or pushed to the ground. You can rise quickly and plan a counterattack. Your best strategy is not to wrestle around on the ground where your weight and muscular strength place you at a disadvantage. Never fall down or let yourself be pushed down if you can avoid it. Stay on your feet and keep moving!

IMPORTANT NOTE ON PRACTICING

Many of the techniques you will practice can seriously injure your partner. This can be beneficial against an assailant, but in practice you want to be sure you will have a partner to practice with in the future! At the same time you want to carry out and complete the move so that you are confident that it will work when you need it.

Can you recall, without referring to the text, the safety precautions you should follow in practicing self-defense reactions?

In practice, throw your punches to within an inch of your partner. Wrist moves and falling techniques should be done slowly at first. Practice in slow motion until you understand how the technique works. Only after you have grasped the techniques should you increase your speed, then concentrate on becoming more effective and efficient.

A certain amount of explanation and understanding are required to learn any physical motor skill. The best form of learning is doing. In any case, immediate response can be critical in a woman's self-defense. You can benefit by suspending elaborate thought processes or conversation with your partner. Concentrate on moving your body as you watch the instructor's example. To learn them, so that they become natural responses, techniques should be repeated over and over. By changing partners frequently you can test your skill with a variety of heights, weights, and body types. This will teach your body to adapt automatically in a real situation.

As a beginner you may want to show a boyfriend, brother, father, or other male the great secrets you are learning in your self-defense class. Only if you have mastered the skills and are willing to hurt these persons will the techniques be successful. For the technique to work the attacker must be committed to a real attack and the defender to a real defense. Because you may not want to hurt your friend he may have an opportunity to overpower or stop you. This may make you feel foolish and lessen your confidence. Rather than submit yourself to this type of discouragement, overcome your urge to demonstrate your newfound knowledge to a male friend.

Practice each technique with your partner four times, alternating left and right sides, then change so that both persons have an opportunity to attack and defend. Practicing on both sides prepares you to respond to any attack, increasing your body balance and equilibrium. Often you will learn easier or more quickly on one side than the other. This is normal. Use the side where you do better in order to understand mistakes you are making on the opposite side, until both become even, smooth, and fluid.

Before practice take off any rings, watches, necklaces, and earrings to prevent injury to yourself or your partner. Wear loose-fitting clothing in which you can move freely and easily. Classes can be held barefooted in a mat room or outside with shoes, on a grassy field. Choose an area where an audience will not form. Onlookers tend to distract your attention, make you self-conscious, and disrupt the class. A class composed entirely of women provides the best atmosphere for initial learning. After gaining some degree of confidence and skill, women will find it necessary to practice with men. To be attacked by a man is a totally different experience from being attacked by a woman. To acquire this experience the instructor can arrange to have men join the class at various times.

Warning

These techniques can be dangerous. Applied in a hap-hazard or thoughtless manner, they could even sprain joints or break bones. Be careful to practice slowly and precisely until you understand the motions. After you feel you understand the proper execution of the techniques, you will realize they are based more on proper timing and surprise than on speed. Continue to practice with safety as a consideration.

Practice these techniques under the supervision of an instructor and if you have any questions ask for more explanation and assistance.

striking
and kicking
5

If you are cornered you will need to carry your assertiveness training a step
further. Some women have fought with brothers when they were young and
are familiar with punching and kicking. Others were taught this was unlady-
like; they have psychological blocks against hurting another person even if it
is in their own defense. Your enrollment in this class reveals a commitment
to overcome psychological obstacles and the results of social conditioning.

Shouting and fleeing may be sufficient to divert or impede an attempted
mugging, rape, or kidnapping. On the other hand, you might face a persistent
attacker, be confronted in a lonely place where help is far away, or be attacked by a mentally unbalanced person. In these cases your defense measures
will need to be more positive.

If you are forced to submit or fight, only you can decide on the correct
course of action. You must weigh the consequences and make a choice on
the most advantageous path to follow. Ask yourself what is at stake: your life
or your property. If your life is threatened, you will want to use every skill,
including violence, to elude the attack.

By learning to be assertive you can make your determination clear in a
confrontation. But what do you do when a man physically forces the issue?
You may need physical effort to make clear your decision to resist.

In the following chapters you will learn to ward off and break holds in
order to avoid being dragged away or knocked down. This may not be enough.
The situation may arise when you need to disable the attacker so as to make
your escape. Learning some basic strikes and kicks will greatly increase your
options when attacked. Your decision to use these counterattacks will depend
upon the attacker, the situation, and your own feelings. You may feel you
would rather not break a hold and run away. This means standing up and
fighting back. If you believe you are basically worth fighting for, your instinct for survival will take over in an emergency. How much you are willing
to suffer threats before counterattacking will determine the measures you use
and how soon you use them.

Fear plays a large role in any confrontation. If they are discouraged from
playing sports and overprotected, women develop a fear of pain because of

their lack of experience. You can prepare yourself mentally for overcoming pain by realizing that pain by itself will not stop you. The fear of being hurt is more damaging that the actual pain of a blow. Once your adrenaline is circulating and you are asserting yourself totally, psychologically and physically, to avoid becoming a victim, your awareness of pain is lessened. You will not feel pain until afterwards.

Some women fear their anger because they have never released it by striking someone. It takes a well-placed, well-coordinated blow to incapacitate someone even temporarily. Don't expect an assailant to give up at the first punch. The more effective your accuracy, timing, and power, the quicker he will realize his assault is not worth the pain you can cause him.

Your objective is not to defeat an attacker in a prolonged fight, but rather to elude him with as little damage to yourself as possible. Many women have reported that men seem matter of fact about a physical assault, and that an assailant is afraid of being caught. He expects you to become a victim, to submit without resisting. He is afraid of being hurt. By counterattacking totally and quickly you can use an attacker's fear to your advantage.

Suprise is your best weapon. Men do not expect women to resist. Even if you are successfully able to slip away from an attempt to grab you, the attacker will not necessarily assume you will strike him. Assuming a fighting stance will eliminate the element of surprise and give the attacker the initiative. If you are smaller and less strong, he may feel his chances are better and decide to fight you. You should not wait too long. After all else has failed or if the alternative is clear, get as close as possible to your assailant and suddenly unleash a counterattack.

Several basic principles will greatly increase the effectiveness of your blows and kicks.

SPEED: Don't wind up or reveal your intention to strike. Speed is essential if the element of surprise is to be effective. A strong blow does not require great muscular force. The strength of a blow is determined by the speed of muscular expansion and contraction. Force is accumulated by speed and is converted to striking power at the end of the movement.

FOCUS: Focus as the word is used here means the mental concentration employed in a blow or kick. When you are under stress you will need to concentrate all of your dynamic willpower and direct it accurately and precisely to achieve the most telling effect. Even great amounts of strength and power will be of little effect if dispersed. Thrashing about or struggling lacks focus. Applying a small amount of strength at one limited point with total concentration is the most effective.

DEVELOPING MAXIMUM POWER: Your arm muscles by themselves are weak. The strongest blow or kick is an extension of the force of the body achieved by coordinating a strike with legs, hip rotation, and proper alignment of the body. The resulting force exerted by a fist will be much greater. Power comes from the hips rotating and thrusting toward a target. Pounding an attacker on the chest will do little good. Striking the attacker in the solar plexus or Adams apple with the full force of your body behind you can incapacitate him.

Certain basic principles apply in striking. Maintain your balance when shifting your weight forward to strike, and do not let the force of your thrust throw you off balance when delivering the blow. Stay relaxed to obtain maximum speed, tensing for a split second at the moment of impact. You should apply dynamic willpower in carrying the motion through so as to develop full power, *striking through* or beyond the target.

Breathing plays an important role in striking. Exhaling on the strike will maximize your power. At the moment of impact use the yell you have developed. Contracting your muscles will add to the suddeness of the attack and increase your power.

Never be satisfied with one defensive blow when two or three can be delivered in rapid succession. If your assailant is strong, mentally disordered, drunk, or drugged, one blow may not be effective. When you are threatened, use whatever force is necessary to incapacitate your attacker. Continue your blows to the same area, or use combinations of blows and kicks until your attacker is no longer a threat.

You will want to take advantage of an assailant's weak points. Many structural weaknesses make the body vulnerable. Pressure or blows to these areas can result in unconsciousness, severe pain, and even death. This does not mean it will happen every time. It may actually be very difficult to place a strong blow in these areas. Nevertheless, a close miss can get results. Study the locations of these vulnerable points (fig. 5.1). When practicing your

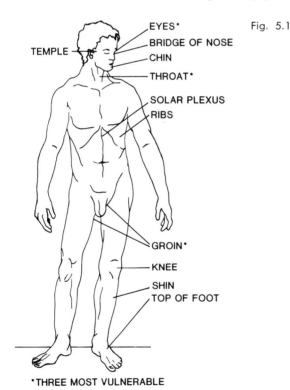

EYES *
BRIDGE OF NOSE
TEMPLE
CHIN
THROAT *
SOLAR PLEXUS
RIBS
GROIN *
KNEE
SHIN
TOP OF FOOT

Fig. 5.1

*THREE MOST VULNERABLE

strikes and kicks, vary the exercises by drawing or taping an X on a strong pillow, a large soft ball, or a football blocking pad so that you can increase your accuracy.

After each strike and kick is perfected, have each person hit the pad with combinations of blows and kicks. Move the target around so you will be able to reach the target without staring at it. Don't concentrate too much on a target that cannot strike back. Remember, in any real situation you too are vulnerable. Your best strategy is to surprise your attacker with short swift blows repeated until he desists and you can flee.

STRIKING

Caution: Don't fold your thumb inside your fingers because you may dislocate your thumb joint when striking.

If you have been seized from the rear and need to disable your attacker, which strikes or kicks might best be tried and which targets are recommended?

BASIC PUNCH

Unless you are used to punching, you can break your hand when hitting a hard object like the skull. To form a proper fist begin by curling your fingers toward their base and rolling your fist closed. Tuck your thumb over the second joint of the first and second fingers (fig. 5.2). This form of the fist can be used to strike soft parts of the body. From your basic stance shift your left foot forward, shoving off with your right foot, and twisting your right hip forward. The full force of the blow should land before your weight is totally shifted to your forward foot. At the same time bring your right fist from your side straight toward the target. Keep your elbow close to your body as you strike. You should remain totally relaxed, tensing your muscles only at the moment of impact. Rather than letting the force of the blow land on the surface of the target, aim several inches into the target itself. As you strike your elbow is extended but not locked, and your wrist is aligned with your forearm. Your back is straight (fig. 5.3). Curling your wrist could cause a sprain. Strike with your knuckles perpendicular to the ground or rotate your fist until the knuckles are parallel to the ground. To achieve the twisting motion of a karate punch, rotate your fist from the perpendicular to the parallel just before impact. *Targets are the soft parts of the body—the Adam's apple, the solar plexus, or groin.*

HEEL OF THE HAND

This blow is easiest for inexperienced people to master quickly. Extend your fingers and thumb upward and bring your wrist back toward your forearm. The striking surface is the soft padding on the heel of the hand (fig. 5.4).

Fig. 5.2   Fig. 5.3

To generate full force with this strike you will need to shove off from the floor with your rearward foot, rotating your hip on the side toward the attacker, while extending your elbow (fig. 5.5). The target is beneath the chin and just below the nose. The full force of the blow should rock the attacker's head back suddenly, leaving him open to a follow-up kick to the kneecap or groin, or a punch to the solar plexus. Practice with each person holding a target at or just above head level. Strike upwards at a 45-degree angle.

SPEAR HAND

Extend your fingers and thumb straight *forward*, keeping the thumb close to the fingers. The tips of the second and third fingers form the striking surface. Use the same hip rotation and body coordination as in the basic punch, keeping the palm roughly parallel to the floor (fig. 5.6). All the force is

Fig. 5.4   Fig. 5.5

concentrated on a very small area, which maximizes your power. Strike for the eyes, the throat, underneath the chin, or the solar plexus. Practice for accuracy and speed rather than sheer force.

HAMMER FIST

Form the fist as the basic punch. The striking surface is the soft pad of the hand along the outside edge of the palm (fig. 5.7). Rotate your hips, placing the force of your body behind the blow as you chop downward. Strike to the groin, the side of the neck or temple, or the nose (fig. 5.8). Strike to the base of the head or to the neck if an assailant is lower than you. Practice with a cushion or pad at different angles and heights so that you understand the most effective use of this fist.

Fig. 5.6   Fig. 5.7

Fig. 5.8

ELBOW STRIKE

Making a fist and bending your arm at a 45-degree angle will help you focus the force of this blow. Use your hips and let your upper body and elbow swing freely when striking. Stay relaxed. Keep your elbow close to your body and bring the fingers of your closed fist to your ear. You can strike to the rear, to the side, or, by using the basic punch stance, you can strike to the front with an upward motion. Targets are the ribs, the solar plexus, the groin, the temple or jaw, the face, or beneath the chin (fig. 5.9). With restraint practice this skill with a partner so as to gauge the proper distancing. Practice with pads when learning to coordinate the power of hips and upper body effectively.

KICKS

In any practical situation, the attacker may be moving. This makes accuracy difficult. A static target is best. Care should be exercised so you don't throw yourself off balance.

Keep all kicks low, striking no higher than the knee. A groin kick is a difficult target because men instinctively protect themselves. Pull your kick back rapidly so that it won't be caught and used against you.

STRAIGHT KICK

Hard-soled shoes are excellent for kicking. Curl your toes back and upward so you will not sprain them when kicking. The striking surface is the ball of the foot. Shift your weight to the supporting leg, maintaining your balance. Raise your knee, moving your foot back. Suddenly snap out from the knee to strike, bringing the foot back before lowering the knee. For added power thrust your hip forward just before contact (fig. 5.10). For speed, concentrate

Fig. 5.9   Fig. 5.10

more on snapping your foot back rather than the kicking outward motion. Practice until you have one smooth, continuous motion. Targets are the shins and the kneecap. Practice for accuracy with a partner wearing pads, and for power practice with a dummy.

Caution: *The kneecap dislocates very easily. Practice carefully and slowly because you can dislocate the knee even when wearing pads!*

STOMPING

The striking surface is the heel of the foot. Bring your knee up as in the basic straight kick. Suddenly slam your foot downward, with the top of the instep furnishing the point of contact. Remember that the bones of the foot are very fragile and vulnerable. Extend the leg fully, striking beyond the foot toward the floor for maximum results. Look at your target before kicking. If you miss the first time, follow up repeatedly. This is an especially good technique if you are attacked from the rear because it comes as a complete surprise (fig. 5.11a). (fig. 5.11b). Practice on a soft surface so that you will not damage your own heel, ankle, or leg.

KNEE RAISE

The knee can be effective at close range only if you make direct contact to the testes. Contrary to popular belief, a groin blow does not disable a man, nor is it easy to strike the groin with the knee. Make repeated knee raises or follow up with foot stomps or strikes. Bend the leg at the knee in a 90-degree angle. The top point of the knee is the striking surface. To increase your power, bend the opposite knee slightly and thrust upwards with your body weight (fig 5.12). Practice by holding a pad at the correct height so that you

Fig. 5.11a   Fig. 5.11b   Fig. 5.12

can instinctively make contact without looking to warn an attacker of your intention.

These kicks and strikes are not meant to be used in an actual fight where blows are exchanged over an extended period of time. They require a minimum of learning for a maximum effectiveness. Practice the counterattacks many times throughout the sessions. Train so that they become habitual actions you can use instantly. Remember, they do not need to be your first response. They are only meant to be debilitating blows when you are definitely threatened with physical harm.

In the following techniques, the descriptions will instruct you as to the best use of blows that are effective with the different types of attacks. Practice the initial releases, attempting to get away first before resorting to the blows. When you are trapped by an assailant, you can more readily deliver the blows. Every attack leaves the attacker vulnerable, open to a strong counterattack. As you train you will learn to observe openings, and once you are familiar with this section you will be able to use the most effective and efficient blows.

releases from body grabs and holds

6

Up to this point we have stressed the initial stages of a confrontation: how to be assertive without being overtly aggressive, how to focus willpower for greater strength, how to avoid potentially dangerous situations, and how to discourage subtle and irritating incidents and prevent them from becoming physical confrontations. Coordinating mind and body will help provide a means of defending ourselves against physical attacks. When your mind and body work together harmoniously, your maximum strength begins to flow unhindered. Coupled with self assertion, this power can often be enough to ward off an attack. If other methods do not work, you need a solid physical technique to fall back on. Although you have practiced the principles of movement, stance, balance, and avoidance, these need to be placed in an active context simulating an actual attack, so that you will have some experience in a realistic situation.

The following section assumes that all means of coping with a potential attack have already been tried. The attacker intends to harm you. If someone threatens you with a gun and demands your purse, give it to him. There is the likelihood that he will leave; and your life is worth more than any amount of money. On the other hand, if you are threatened verbally with rape you have to determine your chances for escape, evasion, or resistance. You may decide to *give in*. Nonresistance is a choice that may be necessary. It does not make you an accomplice to your own rape. It is important not to hate yourself later for not resisting. (If you are raped contact the police immediately to increase the possibility of capturing the rapist.)

Or you can decide to resist. A weak counterattack will only reveal to an assailant that you know how to fight but are indecisive. The element of surprise is gone. Resisting 100 percent means that you are willing to injure or severely maim an attacker.

Techniques to defend yourself from an attack cannot be learned by looking at a book. A technique cannot be taught to respond to every possible attack under all circumstances. To learn the following skills you will have to practice them repeatedly until they become second nature. After you have started the course, begin each class by reviewing one of the earlier techniques. You will like some techniques better than others. It is better to master several escapes, releases, and counterattacks than to learn fifteen or twenty incompletely. Learning to move in an assertive, concentrated, and balanced way will give you a method for dealing with conflict so that techniques can be adapted to new situations. The techniques are derived from the most frequent attacks made against women, and will be an aid in a real-life situation. Their success will depend upon a total commitment and integration of dynamic willpower, knowledge, and body movement.

ESCAPING LUNGES

The use of serious defensive measures does not have to wait until after you have been grabbed. Maintain your basic stance. Keep your crucial distance, being careful not to let your assailant inch forward or box you in. The attacker will need to cover the crucial distance before he can reach you.

Two techniques for escaping from a hold should be used only in extreme circumstances as they may kill your opponent. Do you know what these techniques are and how to practice them safely?

---

1. Your partner will rush forward attempting to grab you around the neck with both hands (fig. 6.1). As he rushes, throw your right hand up to ward off his hands and step forward with your left foot. Push against his upper arm to redirect his force (fig. 6.2). Turn your hips forcefully to the

Fig. 6.1   Fig. 6.2

right, directing your willpower through your arms. Your right leg is firmly placed against the floor and held straight without being locked (fig. 6.3). If you move too soon, your partner can follow your movement and catch you. Wait until your partner is committed toward you before moving. Timing is of critical importance.

2. Your partner is coming to grab you in a bear hug (fig. 6.4). Step forward at a 45-degree angle with your right foot moving to the side of your attacker. As you step, place your forward elbow near your right hip. Using the force of your hips in conjunction with your right hand, catch the partner's elbow from below. Catch the elbow between your thumb and forefinger with your palm facing up. Push the other elbow away with your left hand (fig. 6.5). Push your partner's elbow back toward his face as you pivot suddenly on your right foot, letting your left foot swing to the rear (fig. 6.6). Push the attacker's arm away from you, throwing him forward.

Fig. 6.3   Fig. 6.4

Fig. 6.5   Fig. 6.6

3. An assailant comes at you low to grab one of your legs and throw you to the ground where his size and strength can be used to advantage (fig. 6.7). As he rushes toward you, extend both hands against his upper back. As he grabs for your left leg pivot on your right leg moving your left leg behind you and forcefully pushing him down on his face (fig. 6.8). Guide his forward momentum throwing him on his face rather than attempting to push back into his center of gravity.

4. Your right foot is forward as an attacker rushes forward to grab you. Swing your left hand up to ward off his hands. Extend your right hand to his shoulders (fig. 6.9). Take a step with your right foot to his rear, coming in behind him (fig. 6.10). Your body will be six-to-eight inches from him. Place your hands on his shoulders. Slide your right foot forward another six inches to get well behind him. Suddenly pivot on your foot swinging your left foot in a 180-degree arc to your right. Keep your elbows down but relaxed. Let the momentum from your hips provide the force and pull straight down on your assailant's shoulders, dropping him forcefully to the mat (fig. 6.11).

Fig. 6.7

Fig. 6.8

Fig. 6.9

Fig. 6.10

5. An assailant reaches out and grabs your right shoulder with his right hand (fig. 6.12). Turn your hips slightly toward your left raising your right arm to the outside of his grasp (fig. 6.13). You could strike to his exposed ribs or dart past him to escape (fig. 6.14).

Notes

    a. Turn your head to look in the direction you want to run and your body will naturally follow.

    b. Don't rely on muscle power. Let the force of your hips swing your arms and move your partner.

    c. Check your breathing. You will be breathing heavier but be sure you are not breathing shallowly or taking small breaths.

    d. Make a conscious effort to relax as your partner's hands approach your body. Check to see that you are not freezing, i.e., immobilized by fright.

Fig. 6.11   Fig. 6.12

Fig. 6.13   Fig. 6.14

Additional Practice

As two people walk toward you they suddenly lunge at you. Don't move between them. If you move too soon before they have concentrated on grabbing you, they will be able to catch you. Take the initiative and pivot to the outside, then dart past them to safety. Practice running after you are free and see whether they can catch you. For added effect give a sharp yell as you break their lunge.

ESCAPES FROM HOLDS

Sometimes you are not able to move before an attacker grabs you. Even when the attacker lurches at you, you can use the force of his move without confronting his strength head on. Move quickly when grabbed around the body, because he may try to squeeze the breath from you or throw you to the ground. One of the most common attacks against women is the attempt to overpower them by the weight of the body or by simple brute force. Practice these techniques until your hands move instantly to the vulnerable pressure points. In reacting to all body grabs, whether from the front or rear, let your body relax completely, making it seem like a solid, well-centered foundation. Experiment with this by letting a partner lift you when you are rigid and when you are relaxed. When relaxed your body will be much heavier and feel more "rooted"!

6. Your partner has grabbed you in a bear hug around the body, leaving your arms free (fig. 6.15). Just below both ears at the top of the jawbone is a slight depression where the jawbone connects to the skull. Turning your thumbs sideways place both your thumbs in this depression. Applying even a slight pressure will cause severe pain. Practice on yourself before carefully applying the techniques to your partner (fig. 6.16).

Press your thumbs into the attacker's upper jaw pressure point, directing the pressure to the read of and up into his head at a 45-degree angle. He will release his hold quickly and begin to follow in the direction your hands are pressing. As he releases the hold, he is open for a knee raise to the groin or, if you push hard and fast enough, you can topple him over backwards (fig. 6.17).

Variations: Slap your assailant's ears with the flat palms of your hands. This blow should be used only in extreme cases when you feel your life threatened, as it could kill or result in the loss of hearing. Don't practice except in slow motion.

7. You are grabbed in a bear hug. Clasp the back of the assailant's neck with your left hand (fig. 6.18). Place the inside edge of your right index finger just below the assailant's nose. Exert pressure forward with your other hand, which is back of his head so that he cannot jerk his head away. Push your finger up and back into the nose at a 45-degree angle, forcing the attacker to release his hold (fig. 6.19). Practice until you can apply pressure with either hand without being able to see the attacker's face.

8. An assailant grabs you from the front, constraining your arms by his hold. Let your body relax. Let your dynamic willpower flow along the out-

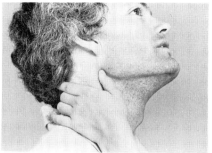

Fig. 6.15   Fig. 6.16

Fig. 6.17   Fig. 6.18   Fig. 6.19

sides of your arms. Expand them outward to give yourself some breathing space. Place your arms around his body and clasp your hands at his backbone (fig. 6.20). Place your chin at the left side of his chest halfway between his shoulder and sternum below the clavicle (collarbone) and just above the heart. Pull with your hands and drive the pointed tip of your chin into his chest (fig. 6.21). Follow up with a knee attack to the groin.

9. Using counterattack techniques is very effective in escaping holds. For an assault that threatens to harm you, more serious measures are often essential. The following variations will incapacitate an attacker, giving you more time to escape than would a mere push.

   a. Grabbed from the rear, stomp sharply on the top of the foot. Bring your knee up and force your heel into the top of the foot, not the

Fig. 6.20 Fig. 6.21

toes. Try to look at your target for more accurate aim. If you cannot see it, keep stomping until you effect a release by hitting the vulnerable spot. If you are unable to raise your knee because you are being held from the front, turn your knee to the outside and stomp. Follow up with a knee attack to the groin.

b. Grabbed from the front, you are lifted off the ground so that you can not kick. Lean your head forward and bite into the tendon above the shoulder or bite the soft part of the neck.

c. When the assailant is about your height and lifts you off your feet you may be able to butt with your head. This works for a rear grab also. Keeping your teeth together and mouth closed, tilt your head back and snap it suddenly forward. Strike with the portion of your forehead at or above the hairline. Striking with your temple is much softer and may knock yourself out. Aim for the bridge of the nose, the teeth, or the cheekbone of your assailant.

REAR GRABS AND HOLDS

The most important aspect of your defense against a rear attack is to not panic. Maintain your balance, keep breathing, and don't become paralyzed. When you practice rear defense techniques, begin slowly from a static position. Gradually work up to the point where you don't know when the attack is coming. Let your partner grab you suddenly. Develop the technique so that you can move swiftly, naturally, and relaxed, as if by second nature in any variety of situations.

A front bear hug, wrist grab, or neck grab may be a playful way to test your responses. The assailant may not be fully committed to an attack. When you can not see an attacker you are in a poor position to judge the situation. To apply your total concentration on retaliation is the safest means of escape. If you are grabbed around the neck you could be choked into unconsciousness or dragged away with slight chance of resistance. A male acquaintaince may be discouraged from a frontal attack by an evasive maneuver, your determination to resist, or your verbal assertiveness. You must judge the severity of your response. It becomes more dangerous for an attacker if he attacks from the rear.

Smashing an attacker's Adam's apple and causing fatal damage would not be justified if you were in a crowded street and were pinched on the bottom. A rear attack that grabs you around the throat even in a semibusy street in the daytime could justify a serious or even fatal injury to the attacker. The first reaction is excessive and based on fear. The second is less impulsive and because of the lack of warning would be considered a legitimate means of self-defense.

10. Begin the practice from a static position, with a partner grasping you in a bear hug. To raise your hands with your palms face up is almost impossible. To affect a release while an attacker is restraining your arms, first move downward with your hands. From the downward position immediately begin to raise your hands rotating them to the inside so the back of your hands face upwards. Let your dynamic willpower run along the underneath, outer (little finger) side of your hands. As you raise your hands make a circle with them in front and slightly above your head level (fig. 6.22).

For greatest effectiveness, this technique should be used before you are entrapped. Your initial response is crucial. As your reflexes improve, increase your speed. The moment you feel an attacker's arms beginning to encircle you, raise your arms as described above (fig. 6.23). At the same time pivot on your forward foot and run past the attacker in the opposite direction.

11. Vary the attack, sometimes having one arm and body encircled and then both arms (fig. 6.24). Let your partner vary his grip also, either holding his own hands at the wrist, interlacing the fingers, or cupping them together. Place your free hand on top of your partner's gripping hand. You will be able to feel his finger without looking. Pry his finger free, encircling it with your

Fig. 6.22   Fig. 6.23   Fig. 6.24

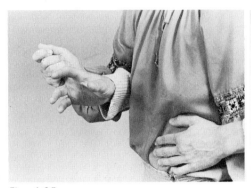

Fig. 6.25

Fig. 6.26

Fig. 6.27

Fig. 6.28

Fig. 6.29

Fig. 6.30

Fig. 6.31

hand. Pull back forcefully, bending the finger toward the back of his hand (fig. 6.25). A heel stomp will distract the attacker's attention if you have trouble prying the finger loose. Once you are free, pivot on your right foot and step free with your left (fig. 6.26). Pull him down backwards or force him to his knees before running away.

Variation: A less damaging release can be obtained by extending the knuckle of your third finger and holding it in a fist. Press against the back of the hand or grind it across the nerves on the top of the hand for immediate release.

12. An attacker grabs you leaving one or both arms free. Step to the left and lower your hips to keep your balance. Bring your elbow up and twist your hips sharply to the rear, aiming for the temple, cheek, or jaw of the attacker (fig. 6.27). When both hands are free follow the multiple response rule. Raise the other elbow and turn in the opposite direction focusing on the opposite side of the attacker's head.

13. As you are grabbed suddenly from behind with both arms trapped, the attacker's momentum pushes you forward. Drop your center of gravity, closing the space between you and your partner. Extend both arms forward (fig. 6.28). Twist forcefully to the right with your hips. Let your right arm go forward and your left arm move rapidly toward your rear, throwing your partner off your back (fig. 6.29). The attacker will fall forward. Do not use a foot stomp, elbow to the ribs, or head butt which will send him backwards; you want him forward. Practice this until you can take advantage of the forward momentum of the bear hug without losing your own balance. Be sure to keep your back straight as you twist your body. Bending at the waist will simply place the attacker on your back (fig. 6.30).

Variation: If the twist does not release his grip, there should be enough space between your bodies to hit with a hammer fist to the groin, or to use a foot stomp or head butt. With this technique and variation you will want to become sensitive to the direction of the force of the attacker. When he pushes, help him along his way to a throw. When he pulls back, move with him, opening the space between your bodies for a blow.

14. An attacker grabs you in a bear hug and raises you off your feet. Relax your body to make it heavier. You should be able to tell where the attacker's head is in relation to your own. Pull your head all the way forward and suddenly butt with the back of your head to the bridge of the nose (fig. 6.31). Use the hard area around the crown for the striking surface. If you use the base of your skull, you could knock yourself out.

RELEASES FROM CHOKES

Choking is one of the most fear-producing attacks. Fear leads to paralysis, fainting, or other self-defeating responses. You can do much to blunt the force of a choke even if you react slowly. Practice until preventing yourself from being choked becomes an automatic, reflex movement.

Fig. 6.32

Fig. 6.33

Fig. 6.34

Fig. 6.35

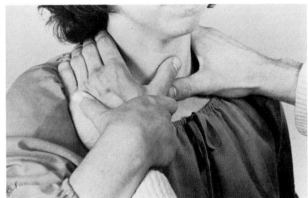

Fig. 6.36

Fig. 6.37

Fig. 6.38

When your head is straight forward your windpipe is exposed. In this position even slight pressure can restrict breathing. The moment you feel yourself being choked or feel hands reaching for your neck, tuck your chin to your chest and turn your head away from the crook of the attacker's arm. Tense the muscles of your jaw and neck, quickly sucking in as much air as you can. Don't yell unless rescue is close by. It's a waste of breath. Practice several times with a partner until you get the feeling of the position of the neck and head (fig. 6.32). Take this protective action for every attempt at choking.

15. As an assailant grabs you with both hands around the neck (fig. 6.33), immediately tuck your chin and turn your head to the side. Bend your knees slightly to keep your balance. Swing your right arm straight up to the outside of the choking arms. Pivot on the right foot, looking over your left shoulder as you move the left foot behind you (fig. 6.34). Power from the hips is transmitted through your relaxed arm to break the choking grip. The attacker is now open to a counterattack, or you may wish to dash to safety.

Variation: When you are grabbed suddenly and cannot move, tuck your chin and turn your head. Reach for the choking hand, catch the little finger and pry it loose from your neck with your thumb. Pull the finger back force-fully, releasing the grip. Follow up with a knee to the groin or other counter-attack.

16. An attacker chokes you from the front with both hands. Tuck your chin, turning your head to the right (fig. 6.35). Place your right palm on top of the attacker's left hand. Grasp the first joint of his thumb and hand with your fingers. Place your thumb at the knuckles between the joints of his little and ring fingers (fig. 6.36). Press the hand held to your neck and turn your hips sharply to your right, dropping to your right knee. As you drop keep your elbow low and bend your attacker's hand back over his wrist as you drop (fig. 6.37). The force comes from your hips. Trying to take the hand off your neck first will be difficult. Let the hand stay on your neck and it will be released instinctively as you drop to the ground.

Caution: In this position you could easily break your partner's wrist by applying enough force at the correct angle. Practice slowly, letting the partner be responsive immediately and go down at the beginning of the pain.

Variation: After grasping the assailant's hand, step back with your left foot, using the force of your hips. Strike his chin with the heel of your left hand (fig. 6.38).

17. When you are held against a wall, or an assailant is especially strong, dropping your weight may not release the grip. You have an excellent target for a knee to the groin or a kick to the shins or kneecap. At the same time

Fig. 6.39b

Fig. 6.39a

Fig. 6.40

Fig. 6.41

Fig. 6.42

Fig. 6.43

Fig. 6.44

Fig. 6.45

extend your right hand between the attacker's arms. Place the tips of your first two fingers at the base of his throat. Curl your fingers downward into this cavity pushing forcefully downward at a 45-degree angle (figs. 6.39a & b). This is an extremely sensitive area. Practice with very slow pressure.

18. Let your partner grasp your throat from the rear with both hands (fig. 6.40). Tuck your chin and turn your head to the side. Step back and to the left with your left foot at a 45-degree angle (fig. 6.41). Retain your balance. Swing both hands to your left side after you bring your right foot back. Be sure to turn your hips all the way to the left. With a sudden rotation of your hips, extend your arms to the right diagonally across your body after you step behind the attacker with your right foot. You will strike the choking arms at the elbow or the forearm in an upward motion (fig. 6.42). By using your body as one solid and coordinated whole, the force of your body weight pivoting on your hips will be enough to knock your partner to the mat.

19. An attacker grabs you around the neck from behind with his forearm around your neck and holds your left hand. Tuck your chin and turn your head to the open side. Move back into your attacker, keeping your center of gravity beneath you. Make a fist and raise your crooked right arm. Forcefully thrust your elbow into his unprotected ribs (fig 6.43). Repeat rapidly several times, retaining your balance. Practice from both sides, making light contact with your partner's ribs.

Variation: Use a finger pull on the hand of the encircling forearm. A foot stomp could be used at the same time.

20. An attacker grabs you from the rear with his right forearm choking you and his left hand holding your wrist (fig. 6.44). Drop your chin immediately, turning your head to the side. Grasp his arm with your fingers looped over the arm and pulling downward close to your body. Bend your left knee slightly and without losing your balance thrust your right leg straight out to your right side (fig. 6.45). Raise your left arm, extending along the outside edge as in number 10. Pivot suddenly to the left, your hips rotating fully. Keep your right elbow close to your body and pull his right arm forward as you pivot (fig. 6.46). The assailant will fall over your outstretched leg.

Variation: Foot stomp to the top of his foot before making the throw.

21. An assailant chokes you around the neck with both hands (fig. 6.47). Tuck your chin to one side. Reach between his arms with both hands to grab his hair. Step back with your left foot, using the force of your hips to pull his head down (fig. 6.48). Pull his head downward by dropping your hips slightly. Bring your left knee forcefully into his face (fig. 6.49).

HAND GRABS AND PULLS

Next to body grabs, wrist grabs are among the most common attacks. An attacker will attempt to pull a woman into a doorway, into a car, or to a secluded spot. The important consideration when being grabbed and pulled

Fig. 6.46

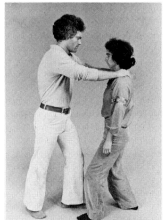

Fig. 6.47

Fig. 6.48

Fig. 6.49

is to not be thrown off balance and placed in a weak position. For a sudden attack when you are pulled forcefully, you should move with the force of the pull until you can recover your balance. Ideally, you want to be able to anticipate an attack and move before you are grabbed.

Sometimes you may be grabbed before you can move. Especially in countering with grabs the practice should be varied. You should keep moving in all situations. At first, respond to a grab from the front. As you progress have the attacks come from the side and from the rear. The defense techniques will also work from a sitting position. Move your body to an advantageous position with the correct distance between you and the assailant so the techniques will work.

Releases from grabs require power from your hips. Your arms acting alone are weaker. With your hips as the stabilized center, direct force through your shoulders and elbows. Hip rotation is more important than pulling with the hips, since pulling will often cause you to fall down or may throw you off balance.

Wrist grabs are readily broken. The weakest part of the grip is the gap between the thumb and the first finger. Turn the narrow part of your wrist to this opening and pull away. If you are grabbed don't tense your muscles. This will make it easier to throw you off balance and drag you away. Fill your arm with dynamic willpower, keep it alive, and feel the connection with your center as you do the technique.

The situation will dictate your response. A release combined with a yell can frighten an attacker away. At a bus stop late at night you need a good counterattack as well as the release. Practice each of the following techniques from a static position, slowly increasing the pulling pressure. As you begin to feel competent in applying the release, begin using counterattacks.

Caution: When forcefully pulling your hands to free them from a grab be careful not to pull them straight back toward your body or face. Move your body so that when the assailant lets go you won't hit yourself. The more effective your release is, the faster it will work.

22. An attacker grabs both your wrists (fig. 6.50). Shift your hips back, pulling the attacker slightly toward you. Bend your elbows slightly and turn the sharp bony part of your wrists into the opening between his thumbs and forefingers. Twist your arms quickly up and to the outside to break the hold. (fig. 6.51).

Variation: If the release doesn't work immediately, kick to the knee and try again (fig. 6.52). After the release works, step forward, pushing off from the ground with the power of your hips. Twist the flat of your palm, thrusting fingers up beneath the attacker's chin.

Fig. 6.50   Fig. 6.51   Fig. 6.52

Fig. 6.53

Fig. 6.54

Fig. 6.55

Fig. 6.56

Fig. 6.57

Fig. 6.58

Fig. 6.59

Fig. 6.60

23. An attacker pulls you forward forcefully, not giving you a chance to step back. Step in the direction of the pull until you have your center of gravity beneath you. Effect the release from a one-hand grab in the same manner as in number 22, following up with an elbow beneath the chin (fig. 6.53).

24. Your right hand is grasped by both hands of an attacker (fig. 6.54). Although your left hand and feet are free, the attacker may assume he can pull you forcefully enough to prevent you from counter-attacking.

Beginning from a static hold, lower your hips slightly. Bend in the knees and not with your back. Lower your elbow and point your fingers to the left of his grip. Extend your dynamic willpower through your pointing fingers. Pivot on your right foot and sweep your left foot all the way behind you (fig. 6.55). Curve your right arm as in technique number 10, and his grip will be broken. If he continues to hold on, continue your pivot toward his rear, keeping the curve in your arm.

Variation: When the attacker releases your arm you will be at his side. Continue your spin, striking at the base of his neck with your left elbow (fig. 6.56).

25. An attacker grabs your right hand in both of his hands (fig. 6.57). Lower your hips slightly and drop your elbow. Point your hand straight up to the outside of his grip (fig. 6.58). Simultaneously, move your left hand just above his elbow. Grasping it between your thumb and forefinger, shift your weight forward and project his elbow toward his nose (fig. 6.59). Slice down suddenly in an arc with both hands. This motion is initiated from the hips, and your body should turn on the balls of your feet. The motion will bend the attacker at the waist and turn him away from you (fig. 6.60). Stepping at a 45-degree angle with your left foot you can push him onto his face. To pin him, force his elbow all the way to the ground and rotate the elbow to the ground.

GROUND RELEASES

Despite all your precautions the possibility exists that you may be thrown to the ground and have an assailant pounce on you. You could be lying down or sitting down and not have time to get to your feet before an attack begins. When your suspicion is aroused don't ignore it. If possible rise from a seated or lying position and maintain a crucial distance until you feel the danger has ended.

In some ways you have a stronger position when you are on the ground because you have a solid base from which to push off. Your mobility and strength, however, are minimized, so that you will need to use leverage to greatest advantage. Don't panic and hopelessly flail about, exhausting yourself. If you remain relaxed and alert you can feel a shift in your attacker's weight, the release of his hands, or his movement to one side. You may be able to force an attacker to relax his guard by talking to him. The moment

Fig. 6.61

Fig. 6.62

Fig. 6.63   Fig. 6.64   Fig. 6.65

Fig. 6.66   Fig. 6.67

you have a clear opportunity, attempt to throw him off. Rather than relying upon one technique, use several. Unless it is a feint, be sure your move is fully committed.

When you are held down by an attacker, you are vulnerable. But there is a split second when he releases your hand and draws back to strike. This may be your only opportunity to effect an escape. Perhaps you will never need to use these techniques, but learn them in case of an emergency.

26. The Crab: You have been pushed to the ground and an attacker hovers over you ready to pounce. Roll onto your left side and lift your head and neck up off the ground, keeping your eyes on the attacker. Place your left palm on the ground (fig. 6.61).

From this position you can slide around on the ground, keeping your legs toward the attacker. Turn to your right side, reversing your arm and leg positions if the attacker moves toward your right. Keep your feet toward the attacker and prepare to kick. Kick out suddenly with your heel if he lunges at you (fig. 6.62). Be careful not to leave your foot extended or he might catch it. If your foot is caught, immediately kick with the other foot. Use repeated kicks. When the opportunity presents itself get up from the ground.

27. You are being straddled and choked while lying on your back. Duck your neck down and to one side taking a deep breath to avoid being choked unconscious. Bring both knees up to the attacker's back and rise onto your toes (fig. 6.63). Place your left hand on the back of the attacker's right elbow and your right hand on the front of the attacker's left elbow (fig. 6.64). Catch with your thumbs so your hands won't slip off. Suddenly arch your back and twist your hips to the right. Simultaneously push with your right and pull with your left arms using a rotary motion as if you were turning a steering wheel. The attacker will fall over your right shoulder (fig. 6.65). Roll toward your left side and rise quickly to flee.

Check: Are you pushing the arms against the attacker's strength? Elude his strength, letting your hands follow the outline of a circle.

28. You are being held by both hands while being straddled (fig. 6.66). Your attacker draws back to slap you. With your left hand immediately reach for the hollow of his throat. Push your fingers up across the bone to find the soft hollow part. Press in and down forcefully (fig. 6.67). At the same time get onto your toes and twist your hips suddenly to the right. Raising your hand to his throat will help protect you from a punch or slap, but you must act quickly. He may release your other hand to protect himself. If so, pound to the groin with a hammer fist or spear to the eyes with your fingernails.

Caution: Practice this technique slowly, applying pressure gradually until you affect a release. Be careful not to injure the throat of your partner. Rolling from the hips will provide more force than mere rolling with the shoulders!

weapons defense
7

Facing a weapon can be a frightening experience. It calls for sober judgment, calmness, and alertness, because your life may be at stake. A weapon immediately limits your chances of success in defending yourself. But unless your life is immediately threatened you should never attempt to rush forward and disarm an assailant. Any aggressive action from you could force him to use a weapon he may have exhibited only to frighten you. Displaying a weapon makes the assailant feel in charge and powerful. Feigning to accept his apparent superiority may give you an added element of surprise.

When facing an armed assailant one of the most important elements to determine is, "What does he want?" If a mugger accosts you demanding money, give it to him. Chances are an armed unknown assailant is not intent on killing you. Your belligerence and resistance could cause him to pull the trigger.

In some situations you don't need to wait around to find out what he wants. If your screen door is locked when you open the front door to find yourself threatened with a knife or gun, you may safely slam the door, ducking out of the line of fire. Such situations require you to remain calm, immediately considering your alternatives and using the opportunity of the moment.

Confronted by a situation where there is no immediate avenue of escape, you will have to weigh the probability of the assailant harming you. How near is help? Can you maneuver to an escape route? Is the assailant drunk or drugged? Is he desperate? Would your shouts or cries discourage him? Would he go away if you gave him money? Are you being kidnapped?

Attempt to talk to the assailant so that you may reduce the unknowns. Appear to comply with his demands, biding your time. Refuse to let him tie you up or place you in a helpless position. You may want to talk to him, go

---

Do you know why it is recommended that you try to talk with an armed assailant?

---

limp, appear to cooperate until the moment of escape, or simply stand your ground. To accompany him or let yourself be tied up means you put yourself at his mercy. He could take you to a deserted spot and injure you. Being injured at a spot where someone would find you quickly is more advantageous.

It is to be hoped that you will never have to face an armed assailant. The most important reason for learning to disarm an attacker is so that you can learn to be more calm than you would be without this training. Such knowledge could be indisposable if you are faced with an armed assailant who you know plans to harm you. In any weapon attack your strategy should be to keep from being injured and placed at the mercy of the attacker. Flee at the first opportunity.

NOTES ON WEAPONS

Unless you have been well trained on a firing range and are completely familiar with a pistol, it is not advisable to rely on a hand gun for your defense. Especially in a confrontation, shooting someone is a difficult act. The tendency is to use the gun to keep an assailant from attacking you. He may know this, and unless you are willing to shoot he can take the gun away from you. Surprising a burglar or assailant with a gun could force him to shoot you out of fear. Moreover, it is illegal to carry a concealed weapon without a permit. Unless you carry a gun on your hip or in your hand it is not readily available in an emergency. For these reasons guns are not recommended as realistic means of self-defense.

Less lethal forms of weapons which shoot bags, wooden pellets, electric shocks, and puttylike substances are available on the market. While not deadly, they may be very useful. However, law enforcement authorities are concerned because they furnish a false sense of security.

Carrying a knife may be regarded as possessing a concealed weapon. Unless you are an expert in its use, a knife can be taken away from you and used against you. Cans of mace, tear gas, or hair spray may not be readily available, and weapons such as hat pins or pencils are not lethal unless aimed at the throat or eyes; if they miss their mark they may tend to anger an attacker rather than disable him. These weapons might encourage you to take chances you otherwise would not take. Rather than using weapons, you should remember that your judgment and foresight are your best protection.

There are many common objects that can be used as nonlethal weapons yet could discourage an attack. It is unlikely that these weapons would be used against you. In any case the purpose of your defense is to escape, and if necessary to incapacitate an attacker so that he cannot follow you.

Several common objects that you might be carrying are suggested in the text as improvised weapons. Can you suggest several other items that might serve the same purpose?

If you are carrying any of the following common objects don't throw them away at the first sign of an attack. Use them to your advantage to surprise and discourage an attacker. The following list of legal, effective common objects enumerates improvised weapons you can use if necessary.

1. Hard covered book: Grasp the book firmly with both hands, then jam the top edge beneath the chin or beneath the bridge of the nose.
2. Car keys: While walking to your car at night you can carry your keys in your hand. Form a fist cushioning the base of the keys against your palm, letting a key protrude between your fingers with the serrated edge down. Slash across the face or eyes, or jab to the eyes or throat or to the soft part beneath the chin.
3. Stiff hairbrush or comb: Rake across the eyes.
4. Umbrella or broom: Hold parallel to the ground and use as a spear to the groin, the solar plexus, or the face. Lunge forward and retreat quickly. If he grabs and holds, kick to the kneecap or the shin.
5. Flashlight: Use as a club at close range. Bring it down to the bridge of the nose or to the temple, swinging it in an arc outside the attacker's line of vision.
6: Purse: A hard purse can be used like a book if it has sharp edges. A soft purse can be swung to distract an attacker. By itself it will not inflict injury. As the attacker raises his hand to block the blow, counterattack to the groin or kneecap with a series of rapid kicks.
7. A rock: A rock concealed in the palm of the hand can be swung to the temple or to the bridge of the nose.

MULTIPLE ATTACKS

The possibility of being approached or attacked by two or more men is a real one. Although you are in an even more difficult situation when facing two stronger and larger assailants, you should remember that fear remains the critical factor. Practicing against two or more attackers can help you overcome this fear and teach you some important moves to ward off several attackers.

When approached by more than one attacker, what are the most important points to remember?

A basic principle when facing several assailants is to never move toward the center of the attackers. Your chances of being grabbed are greatly reduced if you *always move to the outside*. Shift your weight, inch to the side, and attempt always to keep one attacker between you and the others. Once you are grabbed, move to the outside and push or throw one attacker in front of the other. Use an attacker's body just as you would any other obstruction. Don't turn your back so you can be grabbed from behind, but *turn, turn, turn, and keep moving*. If possible, attack the weaker assailant. Disabling one attacker may discourage the others. By yelling constantly and offering strong resistance you may be able to escape from what seems like an indefensible position. After you have decided to move, concentrate your energy fully on one person at a time. When one person is down turn to the next. Only after all of your other means of defense have been repulsed or failed, and you have been stopped, should you rely upon the following techniques.

You are stopped by two men and one reaches out to grab your right shoulder (fig. 7.1). Raise your right hand to the outside of the grip and pivot on your right foot sweeping your left foot to the rear (fig. 7.2). Step back at a 45-degree angle with your right foot as you cut down with your right hand. Turn back into the nearest assailant, pushing from your hips forcefully against his upper arm (fig. 7.3).

One man has grabbed you around the neck and is choking you (fig. 7.4). The other is standing in front reaching for you. Execute the twist throw (number 20, p. 65, tossing one over your outstretched leg and causing him to land in front of the assailant facing you (fig. 7.5). Turn to make your escape. A variation would be to kick to the kneecap of the one in front first before throwing the one in the rear.

Fig. 7.1

Fig. 7.2

Fig. 7.3

Fig. 7.4

Fig. 7.5

THE PRESSURE IS ON

How much have you learned?

Think of as many holds as you have practiced. Have one person hold and another stand nearby or in front. Find as many ways as you can to break the hold and counterattack in such a way so that you can move to the outside and get away.

Let two people rush you at once. Recalling what you have learned, move in such a way as to avoid the grab, keeping one of the attackers between you and the other assailant. Practice at least three variations.

MULTIPLE FREESTYLE ATTACKS

These last two practices will take some thinking. Before planning a response see how many defensive moves come from your natural motions. Only after the spontaneous practice should you figure out variations. Move slowly at first. Share your knowledge with the rest of the class. Have different people think of as many variations and combinations as they can. *Be sure not to injure another student when throwing one person into another.* Choose two or three of the simplest, most natural, and effective variations, then have the whole class practice them.

Suggested variations:

1. Two-hand drop from behind on the free side. (Number 4, p. 54)
2. Bear hug, continuing the pressure (number 7, p. 56) and turning to face the next assailant, or stepping behind the fallen attacker to give yourself room to run.
3. Two-hand choke arm swing (number 15, p. 61), turning to the outside away from the next attacker.

self-defense for health and exercise

8

Whether your purpose is to feel more confident or to master a physical challenge, you will probably find that you feel better after each class session. The human body functions better with exercise. Increased blood circulation, greater lung capacity, and better glanular functioning all have positive and direct effects on how we feel about ourselves and our surroundings. Becoming physically fit will increase your endurance and energy level, allowing you to relax and rest more easily; it should help you to concentrate mentally for longer periods of time.

Have you thought through the outcomes of this self-defense course that are most meaningful to you? Once you have completed the course, how will you maintain your skills, knowledge, and level of fitness?

We have expanded the notions of *self-defense* to include not only the usual defensive measures against physical assault but also defense against accumulating tension, energy-draining emotions, illness, and everyday strain. Physical confrontations and intimidation play a role in fostering these negative reactions. Feeling physically more confident can put your fears to rest.

Exercise and physical activity can have an indirect effect on your ability to defend yourself. Alertness will enable you to foresee and avoid possible assaults. Stamina, endurance, and strength will provide energy to resist an assailant. Physical fitness supplements personal defense and goes beyond it. We recommend you find a regular form of enjoyable exercise in which you can participate for the rest of your life.

If you are physically fit you can return to this book and periodically review self-defense techniques. To get in shape before doing this will require much time and energy. If you have a regular form of exercise and follow a healthy life-style, the moves and techniques can be recalled quickly, and you will feel better in the long run. Centering, balance, coordination of mind and body, projection, and relaxation are all enhanced by daily exercise.

Jogging, bicycling, swimming, tennis, and volleyball are excellent forms of exercise to keep physically fit. On the other hand backpacking or skiing are only feasible periodically. Physicians recommend at least three hours of strenuous physical exercise a week for the average person. You should do some stretching before exercising so as to prevent muscle strains. At least twenty minutes of endurance-type activity like running, brisk walking, or tennis are recommended during each of the three hours.

Overall health practices play an important role in physical fitness. While it is beyond the scope of this book to go into them, several considerations should be part of your overall health plan. Your body and mind function best with regular amounts of rest. Without rest your body becomes fatigued and your mind blurs, impairing your ability to defend yourself. Obesity can have a similar effect. While there is no perfect diet, eating the correct amount of the right foods will greatly improve your overall health, coordination, agility, and speed. If you are determined to protect yourself, you will get proper rest and nutrition.

Some basic movements, the mastery of several techniques, a more positive self-image, and mental alertness to physical defense realities will help a woman defend herself. This course is designed to provide a practical guide to help a woman overcome intimidation and to realize that if she chooses to stand up for herself she does have a chance. She does not have to accept submissively the experience of assault. But how long will these techniques remain in your memory? Although they may have a lasting effect on your psychological attitudes, will the techniques be recalled in a real situation?

Self-defense cannot be learned from a book. Nor can it be learned in four months of easy lessons. While these exercises can prove helpful, they will not prepare a woman to win in a knock-down fight against a larger, stronger man. That is why the emphasis has been placed on short effective techniques for warding off the usual types of attack. The object is to escape an assault with as little harm as possible to yourself. To carry this a step further, you should have a program for systematic self-defense training.

Viewed in a larger context, such training is not only for physically resisting and defeating an attacker. Although many people begin studying the martial arts to learn how to defend themselves physically, they may continue for quite different reasons. To devote an hour or two, three to five times a week learning to defend yourself in case you are attacked is not worth the effort. There should be some deeper purpose.

For some the deeper purpose may come from meditation, from which a person emerges more calm, collected, and relaxed. For others there is the challenge of mastering complex movements and feeling the increased energy in their bodies. And for still others it is the bodily activity of exercise, which makes them feel physically and mentally whole.

Mental alertness can become a continual state of mind after studying a martial art. The simulated self-defense situations in the classroom place the person under the stress of physical attack, so that after this training the daily stresses of living seem inconsequential. Rather than feeling threatened or intimidated, you can accept daily irritations with a more positive state of mind.

Confidence is increased. Faced with an emergency or stress, a woman can relax, exert positive energy, and remain centered within herself.

If you have found this course beneficial in more than merely acquiring the physical skills of self-defense, if you want to deepen and increase those skills, or if you are seeking a more enduring form of exercise with physical and psychological stimulation, you should find a good martial arts school. In this connection there are several considerations. The American emphasis on competitive sports has been combined with the traditional Oriental martial arts in many ways. Some schools emphasize contests, while others stress form as exercise, with little self-defense applicability. Each school has a different feeling and flavor, so that much will depend upon your own needs.

The best way to choose a course in martial arts is to visit several schools. Look in the yellow pages under "judo" to find the schools in your city devoted to the study of such martial arts as Aikido, Karate, Taichi, Kung Fu, or Judo. When you visit the school pay particular attention to the instructor. Although many women instructors are conducting schools and more women are studying the martial arts, most instructors and students are men. You will want to be challenged to learn, but you will also want a supportive atmosphere where you are respected and treated as an equal. Talk to the other women students and observe their attitudes toward the school. Talk to the instructor and evaluate what he says. Will he fill your needs?

Many people choose an instructor solely on the basis of his techniques. Look at the students and see what they are like. Is the instructor able to teach what he knows? Do the students stay with the instructor over a period of time? Does the instructor care for the students and spend time helping them individually? How does the school impress you? Is it comfortable or threatening?

After you locate a school and an instructor, you should find your training more interesting, more exciting, and much more effective. You should become physically more fit as well as more alert mentally. After this type of training you should be much better able to defend yourself against any type of attack. It will carry what you have learned in this course several steps further.

But remember, try to look ahead and to anticipate and prevent situations where you need to defend yourself. Avoid danger, try to elude confrontations, let trouble pass you by. Rather than forcing a mugger to the ground, you should measure your success by your ability to avoid him. It is to be hoped that you will never have to use any of the techniques you have learned. But if you do need them, your alertness and concentration, your determination and training will make them work.

selected references

ALBERTI, ROBERT, and EMMONS, MICHAEL L. *Your Perfect Right: A Guide to Assertive Behavior*. Los Angeles: Impact Publishers, 1970.

AMIR, MENACHEM. *Patterns in Forcible Rape*. Chicago: University of Chicago Press, 1971.

ANDERSON, BOB, ed. *Sportsource: Over 210 Sports, Hobbies, and Recreational Activities*. Mountain View, Calif.: World Publications, 1975.

BERNE, ERIC. *Games People Play*. New York: Random House, 1964.

BLOOM, LYNN Z.; COBURN, KAREN; and PEARLMAN, JOAN. *The New Assertive Woman*. New York: Dell-Delacourt Press, 1975.

BROWNMILLER, SUSAN. *Against Our Will: Men, Women, and Rape*. New York: Simon and Schuster, 1975.

CHO, SIHAK HENRY. *Korean Karate: Free Fighting Techniques*. Rutland, Vermont: Charles E Tuttle Company, 1968.

CSIDA, J., and CSIDA, J. *Rape: How to Avoid It and What to Do about It If You Can't*. Chatsworth, Calif.: Books for Better Living, 1974.

DRAEGER, DONN F., and SMITH, ROBERT W. *Asian Fighting Arts*. Tokyo: Kodansha International, 1969.

DYSON, GEOFFREY. *The Mechanics of Athletics*. London: University of London Press, 1962.

GARFINKEL, PERRY. "Psychological Rape: New Terror for Women." *New West Magazine*, February 28, 1977.

HANCOCK, H. IRVING, and HIGASHI, KATSUKUMA. *The Complete Kano Jui-Jitsu (Judo)*. New York: Dover, 1961 (1905).

HANCOCK, H. IRVING. *Japanese Physical Training*. New York: Putnam, 1904.

———. *Jui-Jitsu Combat Tricks*. New York: Putnam, 1904.

HARVEY, LT. COL. M. G. *Comprehensive Self Defense*. New York: Emerson, 1975.

HENDERSON, JOE. *Jog, Run, Race*. Mountain View, Calif.: World Publications, 1977.

HIRAI, TOMIO. *Zen Meditation Therapy*. Tokyo: Japan Publications Inc., 1975.

HURSCH, CAROLYN. *The Trouble with Rape*. Chicago: Nelson-Hall, 1977.

IIJIMA, REV. KANJITSU. *Buddist Yoga.* Tokyo: Japan Publications Inc., 1973.

KELLEY, C. M. *Uniform Crime Reports for the United States.* Washington D.C.: Department of Justice, F.B.I., 1974.

KOBAYASHI, KIYOSHI, and SHARP, HAROLD E. *The Sport of Judo: As Practiced in Japan.* Rutland, Vermont: Charles E. Tuttle Company, 1956.

LEARN, C. R., and O'NEAL, MIKE. *Backpacker's Digest.* Northfield, Ill.: DBI Books, 1976.

MEDEA, ANDRA, and THOMPSON, KATHLEEN. *Against Rape.* New York: Farrar, Straus, and Giroux, 1974.

NAGAI, HARUKA. *Makko-Ho: Five Minutes' Physical Fitness.* Tokyo: Japan Publications Inc., 1972.

NAKAYAMA, MASATOSHI. *Dynamic Karate.* Palo Alto, Calif.: Kodansha International, 1967.

NEW YORK RADICAL FEMINISTS. *Rape: The First Sourcebook for Women.* Edited by Noreen Connell and Cassandra Wilson. New York: New American Library, 1974.

OKI, MASAHIRO. *Practical Yoga.* Tokyo: Japan Publications Inc., 1973.

OYAMA, MASUTATSU. *Mastering Karate.* New York: Grosset and Dunlap, 1966.

PHELPS, STANLEE, and AUSTIN, NANCY. *The Assertive Woman.* San Luis Obispo, Calif.: Impact Publishers, 1975.

QUEEN'S BENCH FOUNDATION. *Rape: Prevention and Resistance.* San Francisco: Queen's Bench Foundation, 1977.

RUSSELL, DIANA E. H. *The Politics of Rape: The Victim's Perspective.* New York: Stein and Day, 1974.

SAITO, MORIHIRO. *Traditional Aikido, volumes I, II, III, IV, and V.* Tokyo: Minato Research and Publishing, 1974-1976.

SATO, T., and OKANO, I. *Vital Judo.* Tokyo: Japan Publications, 1973.

SAWAI, KENICHI. *The Essence of Kung Fu: Taiki-Ken.* Tokyo: Japan Publications, 1972.

SCHEFLEN, ALBERT E., and SCHEFLEN, ALICE. *Body Language and Social Order: Communication as Behavior Control.* Englewood Cliffs, N.J.: Prentice-Hall, 1972.

SCHROEDER, CHARLES RAY, and WALLACE, BILL. *Karate: Basic Concepts and Skills.* Reading, Mass. Addison-Wesley, 1976.

SCOTT, WILLIAM D. *Chinese Kung-Fu (Kempo): An Introduction.* Rutland, Vermont: Charles E. Tuttle Company, 1976.

SEATTLE-KING COUNTY NATIONAL ORGANIZATION FOR WOMEN. *Woman Assert Yourself! An Instructive Handbook.* New York, N.Y. Perennial Library, 1974, 1976.

SHIODA, GOZO. *Dynamic Aikido.* Tokyo: Kodansha International, 1968.

STORASKA, F. *How to Say No to a Rapist and Survive.* New York: Random House, 1975.

SUGANO, JUN. *Basic Karate for Women: Health and Self Defense.* Tokyo: Trans Pacific Publishers, 1976.

THIFFAULT, MARK. *Bicycle Digest.* Northfield, Ill.: Digest Books, 1973.

TODD, MABEL ELSWORTH. *The Thinking Body.* New York: Dance Horizons, 1937.

Tohei, Koichi. *Aikido in Daily Life*. Tokyo: Rikugei Publishing House, 1966.

Tohei, Koichi. *Aikido, the Arts of Self Defense*. Edited by Morihei Uyeshiba. Tokyo: Rikugei Publishing House, 1960.

———. *This is Aikido*. Tokyo: Japan Publications, 1968.

Too, Jimmy S. *The Techniques of Tae Kwon-Do*. Rutland, Vermont: Charles E. Tuttle Company, 1975.

Tracy, Phil. "Street Crime—A tale of Two Cities, San Francisco: Random Violence as a Way of Life." *New West Magazine*, January 17, 1977.

Tutko, Thomas, and Tosi, Umberto. *Sports Psyching: Playing Your Best Game All of the Time*. Los Angeles: Tharcher, 1976.

Ullyot, Dr. Joan. *Women's Running*. Mountain View, Calif.: World Publications, 1976.

Weinrich, Jo Ann, and Weinrich, David. *A Book of Yoga: The Body Temple*. New York: Quadrangle, 1974.

Yamaguchi, N. Gosei. *The Fundamentals of Goju-Ryu Karate, vol. I and II*. Los Angeles: Ohara Publication, 1972.

questions
and answers

Page

1　Several possible trouble signs are: medicines stored within reach of children, water on floor, glass bottles near edge of counter, and rumpled bath mat or rug.

4　At this stage in your reading, you will need to think up your own suggestions for preventive measures. You will find possible answers as you progress through the text.

6　Four myths are: All women want to be raped; she was asking for it; the usual rapist is a psycopath; and women will be killed if they fight back.
(pp. 6-9)

13　No answer in text.

14　No answer in text.

15　The best choice is "Fire." If you yell while being attacked, the assailant may choke you to quit the noise. (pp. 20-21)

23　No answer in text. The forearm should drop limply.

34　No answer in text. Refer to pages indicated for the pivot. (pp.34-36)

40　Safety precautions are: Stop punches an inch short of target; practice techniques in slow motion; suspend elaborate thought processes and conversation; avoid trying out skills on male friends or family members; remove jewelry; and practice under supervision of instructor. (pp. 40-41)

45　The elbow strike to the ribs, solar plexus, groin, temple, jaw, face, or beneath chin and stomping on the top of the instep. (p. 45)

52　Slapping the ears with the flat of the palms and a hard blow to the Adam's apple. Both should be practiced only in slow motion.
(pp. 56, 59)

72　Talking may reduce the "unknowns" about the assailant's intentions, may delay the attack until help arrives and may give you time to plan your defense. (p. 72)

73　No answer in text. Refer to pages indicated for suggestions. (pp. 73-74)

74   Don't panic, always move to the outside, keep turned to keep attackers in front, and try to keep one attacker between you and the others.

(pp. 74-75)

77   No answer in text. Refer to pages indicated for ideas.   (pp. 77-79)

MULTIPLE CHOICE

1. Social conditioning of women as victims begins in
   a. the schools   c. the family
   b. the movies   d. marriage   (p. 5)
2. Women are trained to be
   a. demure   c. assertive
   b. humble   d. sedate   (p. 5)
3. Amir's study in Chicago found 55 percent of women rape victims
   a. fought back fiercely
   b. screamed and attempted to escape
   c. immediately called the police
   d. displayed what he termed submissive behavior   (p. 5)
4. When you suspect physical violence is about to occur, your first response should be to
   a. pick up a weapon
   b. warn the attacker you know karate
   c. leave immediately
   d. stand your ground and don't give an inch   (p. 6)
5. The only form of harrassment of women that has been extensively studied is
   a. the overly familiar bore at a party
   b. rape
   c. the aggressive salesman
   d. the leering sidewalk lecher   (p. 6)
6. Rape is primarily a crime
   a. caused by women wearing sexy clothes
   b. because men can't control their sexual passions
   c. brought about because of pornography
   d. of assault against women   (p. 6)
7. Rape most often occurs because
   a. all women want to be raped
   b. women asked for it
   c. the woman wasn't able to forsee or prevent it
   d. women feel guilty about saying no   (p. 7)
8. Convicted rapists say they select their victims most often because
   a. they were looking for a victim and the women were defenseless
   b. they found an attractive woman
   c. the victim reminded them of their mother
   d. they couldn't resist the urge to rape   (p. 7)
9. On psychological tests, rapists are revealed to be
   a. psychopaths with violent fantasies
   b. indistinguishable from ordinary men
   c. overwhelmed by sexual deprivation
   d. a sick, sexual deviant   (p. 8)
10. What percent of rapes do most studies reveal are committed by strangers?
    a. 90 percent   c. roughly one-half
    b. 75 percent   d. 25 percent   (p. 9)

11. After all studies are analyzed, it's best to consider that
    a. criminals with prior records commit almost all rapes
    b. given the right circumstances the majority of men are capable of rape
    c. every man is a rapist at heart
    d. pornography creates rapists   (p. 8)
12. The results of most studies show rapes occur most often in
    a. cars   c. movie theatres
    b. abandoned buildings   d. the home   (p. 8)
13. Forcible rapes occur most often during
    a. winter   c. summer
    b. fall   d. spring   (p. 8)
14. Most victims of rapes and attempted rapes
    a. were not seriously injured
    b. became paralyzed by fear
    c. immediately tried to scream and run away
    d. were beaten unconscious   (p. 9)
15. The Queen's Bench Study found that in most rapes
    a. struggling was impossible
    b. violent rapists can never be resisted
    c. victim resistance is highly correlated with deterrence of sexual assault
    d. if resistance appears to be futile, it is   (p. 9)
16. The most important obstacle to women defending themselves is
    a. small size and lack of physical strength
    b. fear and intimidation
    c. the fact that others won't come to the rescue
    d. unlighted public streets   (p. 10)
17. The initial steps in changing a person's self-image includes which of the fol-
    lowing?
    a. Confidence you have the ability to change.
    b. A desire to change.
    c. Constant support from your family and friends.
    d. Determination to see yourself in a new way.   (p. 11)
18. The best way to defend yourself when threatened with physical assault is
    a. to carry a gun in your handbag
    b. to thoroughly master boxing and judo
    c. dress in a disguise so men can't tell you're a woman
    d. to anticipate dangerous situations and avoid them   (p. 11)
19. If you were in a situation where you had to defend yourself,
    a. it's best to not think about it until it happens
    b. think about it and plan what you would do beforehand
    c. memorize the phone number of the police
    d. realize there isn't much you can do about it   (p. 12)
20. If you were held up by a nervous gunman who demanded your purse, the
    safest response is to
    a. give it to him
    b. immediately begin screaming, "thief, thief."
    c. grab hold of the gun and take it away from him
    d. throw your purse at him and run   (p. 13)
21. A woman will be better able to anticipate danger to herself if
    a. she stays away from crowds
    b. she minds her own business and doesn't talk to strangers
    c. she keeps her eyes on the sidewalk and doesn't notice men
    d. she is aware of dangerous people and places   (p. 14)

22. If you are in a heated argument with a family member and fear violence, the worst thing you can do is to
    a. stand up for your rights and don't budge an inch
    b. defuse the situation and try to calm the other person
    c. call for help or leave the scene
    d. later call in someone to negotiate   (p. 14)
23. In most cases of reported rape, women had the feeling that
    a. everything would work out okay in the end
    b. something bad was about to happen
    c. they were embarrassed about being so calm
    d. someone would come to their rescue   (p. 15)
24. If a woman facing an armed rapist at her door slammed the door in his face, she would be
    a. making a serious mistake by angering him
    b. only delaying the inevitable
    c. taking the opportunity of the moment to escape
    d. forcing him to shoot her through the door   (p. 15)
25. Being passive, submissive, and at another's mercy leads a woman to
    a. escape possible confrontation because others won't notice her
    b. feel bad, lose self-confidence, and become more anxious
    c. face old situations in new ways
    d. gain respect by not challenging other's authority   (p. 17)
26. When a man you work with but don't trust asks you to go out with him for a drink, the assertive response is to
    a. you should become angry and tell him what you think of him
    b. go with him so you can learn to like him
    c. decide he's not really so bad if he asked you out
    d. tell him firmly but politely you don't want to go   (p. 18)
27. Assertive behavior is a good way to
    a. release anger, hostility, and self-righteousness
    b. dominate and humiliate people you don't like
    c. use intimidation to get something you want
    d. stand up for your rights without violating the rights of others   (p. 18)
28. By building up anger and becoming more aggressive, a woman can
    a. relay to others that she feels good about herself
    b. begin to notice and become sensitive to another's anger
    c. express needs, feelings, and ideas at the expense of others
    d. make others like her by showing she won't be pushed around   (p. 18)
29. Body movements, facial expressions, tone of voice, and other body language accounts for
    a. well over 80 percent of all interchanges
    b. over half of most communications
    c. about 10 percent of our expressions
    d. an insignificant amount of human communications   (p. 19)
30. The best way to use your voice in self-defense is to
    a. cry and plead for mercy
    b. use your voice as a powerful weapon to stun and surprise
    c. yell rape as loudly as you can
    d. begins screaming to frighten the man off   (p. 20)

31. Physical techniques of self defense
    a. are always valuable when someone challenges you
    b. will help you become a better person
    c. can never replace your judgment in avoiding danger
    d. can force men to respect you   (p.21)
32. Those who have successfully escaped rape attacks
    a. are damned lucky
    b. knew how to run fast and scream loudly
    c. waited until it was almost too late
    d. are more physically assertive and employ many techniques   (p. 22)
33. Of all the muscle groups in your body, your hips
    a. should remain locked so you don't lose your balance
    b. maintain body balance
    c. used with balance and extension, multiply arm and leg power
    d. in combination contain the strongest muscles in the body   (p. 25)
34. The most efficient self-defense techniques are designed to
    a. confront power with power
    b. rely upon kicks and punches
    c. be able to last in a long, drawn-out fight
    d. upset the attacker's balance and avoid direct confrontation of power
    against power   (p. 25)
35. Self-defense responses are most effective when
    a. they become subconscious reflexes
    b. you can think about them before you act
    c. you have a chance to warm up first
    d. they rely upon physical strength   (p. 27)
36. When you are facing an attacker, it's best to
    a. look him straight in the eye
    b. watch his hands in case he tries to grab you
    c. take him in with your overall view
    d. focus your attention on your escape route   (p. 32)
37. If a suspicious person approaches you, you should
    a. stay close so he does not surprise you
    b. keep appropriate distance just beyond his reach
    c. become alert to obstructions for your defense
    d. immediately look for escape routes   (p. 33)
38. Special things to consider when beginning practice is
    a. don't commit yourself because it may not work
    b. never practice in slow motion because it will slow you down
    c. talk about the technique till you thoroughly understand it
    d. commit yourself 100 percent and suspend elaborate thought processes
                                                            (p. 40)
39. The best way to learn self defense techniques is to
    a. discuss them with your friends
    b. practice proper technique over and over
    c. suspend elaborate thoughts and discussions
    d. change partners often to test your skills   (p. 40)
40. After you've had a few classes you should
    a. try the techniques on your father or boyfriend
    b. hang out at bars so you can show what you've learned
    c. use the techniques only when necessary
    d. realize you can't master the techniques and quit   (p. 40)

41. Practice in such a manner that you
    a. learn the proper execution of the techniques slowly
    b. realize safety is a prime consideration
    c. realize timing and speed comes with mastery
    d. allow your partner to worry about safety   (p. 41)
42. One of the most important factors in self-defense is
    a. the element of surprise
    b. good boxing skill
    c. a concealed weapon
    d. knowing you don't have a chance   (p. 43)
43. Coordination of which of the following factors is important in punching?
    a. Speed
    b. Focus
    c. Keeping your wrist relaxed and limp
    d. Coordinating your whole body   (p. 43)
44. If you punch or kick an attacker it is best to
    a. rely upon one strong blow
    b. hit him once and run away
    c. use two or three blows in rapid succession
    d. try not to anger him too much   (p. 44)
45. The most vulnerable parts of a man's body are
    a. ribs, knees, and temple
    b. chin, neck, and forehead
    c. foot, elbow, and back
    d. eyes, throat, and groin   (p. 44)
46. Which are important considerations when kicking?
    a. Always kick to the groin.
    b. Main targets are kneecap and shin.
    c. Bring your foot up from the ground.
    d. Keep your toes straight out.   (p. 48)
47. Success in defending yourself depends upon which of the following?
    a. Moving in a balanced, centered, and assertive way.
    b. Overcoming your own fear.
    c. Rely upon three good techniques.
    d. Practice until the moves become second nature.   (p.51)
48. If you're attacked and wind up on the bottom, it's best to
    a. relax until you can use leverage to your greatest advantage
    b. struggle and keep struggling
    c. always give up immediately   (p. 56)
    d. never surrender even if your life is in danger
49. The most important thing to determine when facing an armed attacker is
    a. what he wants
    b. how he's going to kill you
    c. how much he is totally in charge
    d. how belligerent you can be   (p. 72)
50. The first thing to do when someone hands you a gun is to
    a. pretend you know all about it so he won't think you are stupid
    b. immediately check to see if it's loaded
    c. pull the trigger to see if it's loaded
    d. treat it like it's loaded, even after you check it   (p. 73)

51. If you're attacked by several men, it's best to
    a. move toward the middle to show them you're not afraid
    b. turn, turn, and keep moving
    c. turn your back and try to run away
    d. always move to the outside   (p. 74)

QUESTION ANSWER KEY

Multiple Choice

1. c	12. d	22. a	32. d	42. a
2. a, b, d	13. c	23. b	33. b, c, d	43. a, b, d
3. d	14. a	24. c	34. d	44. c
4. c	15. c	25. b	35. a	45. d
5. b	16. b	26. d	36. c	46. b
6. d	17. a, b, d	27. d	37. b, c, d	47. a, b, d
7. c	18. d	28. c	38. d	48. a
8. a	19. b	29. b	39. b, c, d	49. a
9. b	20. a	30. b	40. c	50. b, d
10. c	21. d	31. c	41. a, b, c	51. b, d
11. b				

index